CONCILIUM

Religion in the Seventies

CONCILIUM

Religion in the Seventies

Volume 62: Liturgy

LITURGY IN TRANSITION

Edited by
Herman Schmidt, S.J.

Herder and Herder

1971
HERDER AND HERDER NEW YORK
232 Madison Avenue, New York 10016

Cum approbatione Ecclesiastica

Library of Congress Catalog Card Number: 70–129761

Printed in the United States

CONTENTS

Editorial

ON 7 December 1965 Vatican II promulgated as its final document a pastoral Constitution on the Church in the contemporary world, with the opening words "*Gaudium et Spes*". Because of his intervention in the Council on 4 December 1962, Cardinal Leo Suenens may fairly be called the spiritual progenitor of this Constitution. His intervention took place just when the Council had in principle approved the Constitution on the Sacred Liturgy, although it was not officially promulgated until 4 December 1963. Already during the Council active steps were taken—beginning with Paul VI's *Motu proprio* of 25 January 1964—to implement the Constitution on the Sacred Liturgy. Although this Constitution could not reap the benefit of *Gaudium et Spes*, it is undeniable that it is centred on the world of our time and that the programme needed for carrying it out has *Gaudium et Spes* as its source of inspiration and guidance. The liturgical renewal is in fact an outcome of the way things are developing in the Church and the world at the present time.

In its fifth section the fourth Assembly of the World Council of Churches, meeting at Uppsala from 4 to 20 July 1968, examined a draft document "The worship[1] of God in a secular age", which was inspired by current theological trends in Germany, Britain, The Netherlands and North America.[2] During discussion it came

[1] In the different languages the words "liturgie, cultus, worship, Gottesdienst, eredienst" have their own peculiar shades of meaning which cannot be reproduced in translation, and yet must not be overlooked.

[2] *Drafts for sections prepared for the fourth assembly of the World Council of Churches, Uppsala, Sweden 1968* (Geneva, 1968), pp. 96–111.

under heavy fire because of the "secularizing theology" of Gogarten, Robinson, Hoekendijk, van Leeuwen, van Buren, Cox, and so forth. Eventually, a revised document entitled "Worship" appeared, in which after an Introduction the first chapter was headed "The challenge of secularization".[3] At the same time the Assembly gave Faith and Order a mandate to press on with its examination of "worship".

With that in view Faith and Order held a consultation, from 8 to 13 September 1969, on "Worship in a secularized age".[4] The forty participants were chosen to represent the most divergent tendencies, so as to bring out opposite points of view. The word "secularization" was again chosen—quite deliberately—with the idea of finding out whether this concept really does characterize the "present". Interesting and relevant though the contributions and discussions may be in themselves, the result is more than anything else witness to a sort of distraction, a sense of being here, there and everywhere. The problem of worship brings Christians of various traditions together as *an inquiring and questing fellowship*. The remarkable thing is that in this discussion the dividing lines do not coincide with those of the various Churches, they are thoroughly tangled up. The following came as something of a revelation. Ecumenical dialogue had up to this point been primarily concerned with "ways of worship" in the various traditions. It had been assumed, consciously or unconsciously, that praying is the same in all traditions. The consultation showed that this is not the case. Not that praying together is problematical—but the theoretical issues centred around prayer and worship, these are the problem. Nowadays Christians of varying traditions encounter one another in a closer fellowship; but at the same time they become aware of new polarities. They discover that the problem of unity is posed in a new way. There has been talk of three groups who were in evidence at the consultation: those who *a priori* accept God, Gospel and Church as a given *certainty*, and make this the basis for their religion; those who eschew any

[3] *The Uppsala report 1968; official report of the fourth assembly of the World Council of Churches. Uppsala, July 4-20, 1968*; ed. N. Goodall (Geneva, 1968) pp. 74-85.

[4] The recommendations of the Consultation are published in *Studia Liturgica* 7 (1970), nos. 2-3. A detailed report has been supplied to the participants by Lukas Vischer.

kind of *security*, so that they can be really open and questioning; those who see *uncertainty* and *insecurity* as the true expression of faith and have determined to stand by that uncertainty at all costs. But what do we mean by "certainty" and "security"...?

These circumstances provided the editors of the section on liturgy occasion to study the same problem in more detail. Moreover, there was a special reason for doing so. The fact that the official liturgical books are now ready does not mean that the process of renewing the Church's liturgical life is complete: "We are faced with the most responsible, difficult and important task in the whole process of reform. The new *Liber Sacramentorum* [Roman missal] is now a reality. Pastorally speaking, it still has to be *made* real. This crucial task will come to nothing in the end unless it can be implemented 'in spirit and in truth'. We have somehow to imbue it with life".[5] The revised liturgy is very much part of a general development affecting the Church and the world, which one has no hesitation in describing as critical. It is not surprising that despite certain signs indicative of renewal our liturgical life too is undergoing a crisis. To offer a diagnosis of it is extremely difficult. One even has to admit that initially it has produced more bewilderment than depth or clarity of insight. There is, for instance, a Babel of voices and opinions with regard to the meaning of the following terms: religious and Christian; natural and supernatural; immanent and transcendent, horizontal and vertical, holy (*sanctus*), consecration, ordained (*sacer*), sacral, profane, desacralization; earth, world, secular, secularization, secularizing, secularism. There is a big danger of getting lost amid the complexities of concepts and terminology, so that one is never able to get down to discussing the subject itself: that is, the concrete situation of the liturgy in the world of today.

After some fruitful discussion by correspondence the editors fastened on the theme: "Liturgy of the modern Christian". The

[5] A. Bugnini, "La riforma liturgica verso il porto; il nuovo 'Missale Romanum' ", in *L'Osservatore Romano*, 13-5-1970. Original text "Siamo di fronte all'opera più impegnativa, laboriosa e importante di tutta la riforma. Il nuovo *Liber Sacramentorum* è ormai una realtà. Ora bisogna attuarlo nel ministero pastorale. A nulla infatti sarebbe valso questo importante lavoro, se ora non diventasse 'spirito e vita'. La vita dobbiamo dargliela noi."

authors' intention is to list and interpret as concretely as possible the obstacles which the liturgy finds present in the world of today and, conversely, the world encounters in the liturgy as it is celebrated. In that way they hope to make possible some cogent pronouncements, realistic solutions and guiding principles relevant to the existing situation. This number is intended simply to give a little help in a modest way. It points its readers to this and that aspect in the hope that they will go on thinking things out for themselves. And if we have not so far had any luck with that....

In his approach to the Christian mystery the specialist in liturgy will seek to understand it as it is apprehended and celebrated in Christian congregations, each in its own fashion integrated into the one (albeit pluriform) world. Archaeology and theological expertise are not going to take him far enough. He is bound to inquire how there come to be vital points of contact between Christ as he now lives and people as they now live. The Word of God must be proclaimed through the Scriptures in such a way that it becomes intelligible to each congregation and speaks with a prophetic resonance amid our problems. Liturgy is a proclamation of the Word that became flesh and so is a kind of symbolic activity in accordance with a richly varied ceremonial; the anthropological study of human gestures has shown how very important symbolic activity is in regard to religious expression, having often a richer content than words or any written material. Now that the Roman liturgy is celebrated in all languages, the symbolic ceremonial, as in the Eastern rites, takes on a new value: that of a universal language. Religious ritual is a precious element contributing to man's psychological equilibrium; in the rite he must be able to give expression to his profoundest feelings, so that they are not thrust aside and suppressed. Liturgical ritual, therefore, has to be integrated with life in such a way that through the liturgy a man can really find and conserve his Christian self-identity in his world. In the liturgy the process of symbolizing and identification is impossible except in some relation to a celebrating congregation: nothing can be "expressed", if the assembled people are not one in their thinking and feeling, in faith, hope and love—hence the problems raised by the relations of liturgical observances to the universal Church and individual

Churches, to the local and the Christian congregation, to the parish and the various sorts of groups. If liturgy falls within the realm of "art", then it might be described as the "poetry" (from *poiein*) of religion: at all events it is a creative celebration on the part of the entire congregation, a "folk art", and not the "Art" of the sacramental minister alone. Churches and meeting-places are there in order to create an environment in which the celebrations can proceed freely and naturally, so that one might even speak of a "*milieu divin*". Last of all, it is of the utmost importance that the liturgy be adapted to the mental outlook of a world dominated by the natural sciences, technology, labour, commerce and consumption. Because those who are responsible for the wording and structures of liturgy themselves live in the world of the humanities, they must be very much aware of this fact; so that to reach the Christian where he is and to bring him where he has to be Christian means are employed, and no forced culture is tolerated.

Anyone who cares to go into a large bookshop will there make a discovery. He will find a department full of expensive, carefully produced volumes on the occult sciences, witchcraft, demonology, astrology, I-Ching, parapsychology, Tarot packs, various forms of Eastern mysticism, and so on; if he goes to the paperback section, he will find there the same thing in a popular form. Let him simply look around, and he will discover the strangest outpourings of occultism, superstition, pseudo-religions, meditation centres, the youngsters' underground hang-outs, and so forth. God may have died in the 'sixties (although it does not seem to have happened yet); but with the 'seventies gods and devils rise anew. In the wake of the gloomy 'sixties a more relaxed period would seem to have arrived, with its round of festivity, humour, sarcasm, this frolic and that. If the signs are to be trusted, the 'seventies should present liturgy with fresh opportunities. We all know that groups, spontaneous, inventive and gay, are "doing liturgy" here, there and everywhere. The serious and strait-laced frown in sheer alarm at the excesses and absurdities. Others again resort to self-criticism: is not the official liturgy too dull, too cerebral, too rigid? Is it a game, a form of spiritual refreshment, a beneficial relaxation? From the literature we pick a couple of books here. Peter Berger once more bears the angels and discovers the supernatural in modern society.[6] And from Harvey Cox we have the feast of fools, a theological disquisition on festivity and fantasy.[7] Acquainting himself with this literature is a useful thing for the specialist in liturgy to do. *Homo ludens*, concerning whom Huizinga was writing as early as 1938,[8] is coming into vogue, now that *homo faber* seems not to have enjoyed the success predicted for him. Evidently, something is happening in the secularized world which may well put new pep into our liturgical life and is perhaps opening up for it unprecedented, unfamiliar prospects.

HERMAN SCHMIDT
DAVID POWER
HELMUT HUCKE

[6] P. Berger, *A Rumor of Angels; modern society and the rediscovery of the supernatural* (Garden City, N.Y., 1969).

[7] H. Cox, *The Feast of Fools; a theological essay on festivity and fantasy* (Cambridge, Mass., 1970; 2nd ed.).

[8] J. Huizinga, *Homo ludens; proeve eener bepaling van het spel-element der cultuur* (Haarlem, 1951; 3rd ed.).—Deserving of mention is the little book: E. Trueblood, *The Humour of Christ* (London, 1965).

Translated by Hubert Hoskins

PART I
ARTICLES

Herman Schmidt

Liturgy and Modern Society—Analysis of the Current Situation

FOR purposes of this article I am assuming that the reader is familiar with the problems centring around "secularization" and "desacralization" and with the relevant literature. I am supposing therefore that I can allow myself the liberty of presenting, without any elaborate display of factual information, a concise analysis of the problems raised by the liturgical life and activities of a Church and a society both of which are passing through a phase of complex transition.[1] By applying a number of sharp distinctions and critical interpretations in that analysis I shall try to shed some light on a phenomenon not easy to survey in brief compass. I am well aware of the danger of oversimplifying and of just throwing off a few bald assertions where one might look for a subtler and more qualified set of arguments. In writing this introductory article I had before me the contributions which in this same number elaborate in detail what I can only touch upon here in cursory fashion.

I. A Bird's-eye View of some History

Western culture is fairly represented by a model which despite certain shifts and changes and motley variations has persisted down the centuries. According to this model human existence

[1] On the relevance of the liturgy to the "secularization-desacralization" issue and its problems see L. Maldonado, *Secularizacion de la liturgia* (Madrid, 1970), *Revista di Pastorale Liturgica* 7 (1969), no. 34; *Rivista Liturgica*, 56 (1969), nos. 5–6. A detailed bibliography is provided there.

falls into two sectors, of which one is specifically religious, spiritual, *sacral*, and the other specifically non-religious, profane and *secular*. After the Peace of Constantine the first sector was christianized. In the course of the Middle Ages the religious sector came to dominate, tutor and determine the secular one to such an extent that Western culture became typically Christian. A side-effect of this was a certain under-valuation of earthly things, as witness the liturgical *"terrena despicere et amare caelestia"*,[2] seen in conjunction with various symptoms of "contempt for the world".[3] In the sixteenth century the mundane sector began to gain its independence. With the Renaissance and the growth of Humanism the culture became non-ecclesiastical—which is not *per se* the same as anti-ecclesiastical. It was soon drowned by the noisy and triumphalist clamour of baroque, the last great Christian cultural style in the West. When this was finally silenced (for want of breath), the Church was suddenly confronted during the century of the Enlightenment with the vitality of the mundane sector: the culture was now democratic, based on the exact sciences and a-Christian, although not *ipso facto* anti-Christian. With the enormous successes scored by the sciences and by technology modern culture has become increasingly autonomous: man comes of age and develops the world on his own lines, so that society becomes something a-religious—which is not to say anti-religious.

During the last century the Roman Catholic Church embarked on a process of internal renovation, initially with some success. It looked back nostalgically towards its old medieval styles of culture and tried to revivify by restoring them in a spirit of Romanticism. The Protestant Churches looked for new ways to follow; and various schools of theology emerged, ranging from fundamentalism to liberalism. Towards the modern world the Churches adopted a defensive attitude: they kept themselves to themselves

[2] P. Bruylants, "Terrena despicere et amare caelestia", *Miscellanea Liturgica in onore di S.E. il Card. Giacomo Lercaro* (Roma, 1967), II, pp. 195–206.

[3] *Le mépris du monde* (Problèmes de Vie Religieuse, 22) (Paris, 1965). In the course of the days on which this subject has been studied and handled, J. Leclercq wrote a "Postface" (pp. 55–8) in order to warn us against one-sided notions; a demonstration, therefore, that even today contempt for the world still exists.

in an effort to protect the faithful from the "wicked world". Using an old legal term, they proceeded to talk about "secularization". After the Second World War some churchmen became increasingly aware that Christianity was in danger of shutting itself up inside a ghetto and that it would be out of the question to build a Christian culture that enjoyed the hegemony of earlier periods. Thus there has struggled to emerge a theology of secularization, which seeks to examine, critically and methodically, the complicated development of the modern world and the real character of an historically conditioned Christianity.

In the history of Western culture, the liturgy has had a special position. We are here concerned with a process that began with the Council of Trent. For many reasons—but chiefly because of the Reformation—in the matter of texts, ceremonies, discipline and specific observances, Rome set about the business of fixing her liturgy in the finest detail and, having made it utterly uniform, of wielding her supreme authority to impose it (with a few exceptions) throughout the Latin Church. One result of this was that the liturgy came to stand outside the various currents of cultural evolution and to be in some respects "otherworldly". In that way the Church became an unassailable sacral power face to face with the growing attraction of the mundane sector. Within the Church the liturgy was honoured as the formal act of worship of the "universal" Church, as an *"opus operatum"* of grace and an hierarchical clerical institution. Repeated attempts to integrate the liturgy as a vital pastoral factor in the spiritual life of the faithful came to nothing, chiefly because the groups aiming at such a reform were numerically weak, liturgy had no real place in scholastic theology and the clergy's encounter with it was a form of rubricism. When in the first half of this century the liturgical movement grew stronger and Popes Pius X, Pius XI, Pius XII and John XXIII gave it their support and encouraged its development, the process of renewal was still blocked by powerful opposition. At last the moment of breakthrough came with Vatican II. In the space of a few years so much has been achieved—and with such energy and determination—that even the secularized world is showing a degree of interest. Despite this on balance very positive outcome, there is still a feeling of disquiet and questioning: have we really succeded in giving the liturgy that cultural content and structure which should make, pastorally speaking, an impact on the modern world? However disagreeable this question may be, it can and should be asked, since it does not burke the critical issue of the Church and the world. The problems raised by secularization and desacralization affect the very heart and centre of the liturgy.

II. Secularization[4]

1. The Churches' resistance to what they have called the "secularized" modern world is not infrequently aimed at *what man has achieved in the sphere of science and technology*. It is a sign of weakness, an inferiority complex and, at bottom, an (unconscious) failure to appreciate God's activity in creation; it is a distortion of the mystery of the Incarnation, an attack on human dignity, and suggests a lack of realism. Here is something worth bearing in mind: again and again the Church is obliged to revise its attitude towards science and technology: what it first of all prohibits it later proceeds to accept. This defensive attitude is now dying out—after a protest was uttered at Vatican II, citing what has come to be the classic case of Galileo, and a positive stance was adopted with the Constitution *Gaudium et Spes*.

In the liturgy what was *démodé* and other-worldly was accepted because it was felt to be a token of the sacral. Here too Vatican II ushers in a change, despite obstinate resistance. The mass media made their presence felt, modern musical instruments are heard, new community structures are put to use, works of art, buildings, even utensils, accord with modern taste. To integrate mundane values into the liturgy is to christianize the sphere of human labour, the whole realm of man's work: in this way the dimensions of creation, incarnation, eucharist and resurrection find a more effective expression by being brought within close range of the ordinary Monday-to-Saturday round, as John Robinson argued so suggestively back in 1958.[5]

2. What is described as "secularization", however, implies more

[4] A. Nijk, *Secularisatie; over het gebruik van een woord* (Rotterdam, 1968). It is the most comprehensive synthesis of the whole range of problems, accompanied with a very extensive bibliography.

[5] J. Robinson, *On being the Church in the World; essays* (London, 1964, 3rd edn.), pp. 31–71: "Matter, power and liturgy".

than all this. It is by *man* that the world is changed through the sciences and technology—and changed in so radical a fashion that this same *man* automatically changes his posture or his culture (*debita operatio circa aliquid adhibita*). It is *man* who on his own initiative and in his own strength manipulates his world; and quite of his own accord he conducts himself in that changed world in such a way that as *man* he is perfected through his labour and is not brought down by the new powers and energies that he has released. The following points may be regarded as typifying secularization as a *socio-cultural phenomenon*:

(a) The world is not apprehended as something purely static, but primarily as an historical affair or an evolutionary process: it is a reality to be made, to be constructed and to be created. From *homo contemplativus* (who accepts the world as a spectator) the emphasis shifts to *homo faber* (who experiments and makes the world).

(b) The world is envisaged not just as an expanse (*kosmos*, *mundus*) in which man is more or less happily situated, but first and foremost as a *current of time* (*aion*, *saeculum*), in which man guides or directs the course of events. The accent shifts from *homo staticus* to *homo dynamicus*.

(c) The emphasis is placed on the *future*. Man is all the time making the world anew. For him the world is not something already given; nor is it pre-existent, even though up to a point its evolution is of course conditioned and made possible by the past and the present. Critical and self-reliant, set in the present with his gaze directed to the future, he gives the past its continuing life. From *homo conservativus* the accent shifts to *homo progressivus*.

(d) Secularized man is deeply conscious that in the world-process he has a responsible task and mission to fulfil. He feels especially strongly impelled to promote the typically human values: justice, solidarity, freedom, equality, the dignity of the human person—and all this focused on the building up of a new world, a humanity of the future. Thus his stance over against the existing situation is a critical one; and he creates plans for the future, not only in the technological, scientific and economic spheres but more particularly in a social and political context.

He opposes injustice and alienations in society and does not shrink from launching political and social revolution. He moves from a cosmo-centric to an anthropocentric posture, he struggles against every attempt to manipulate people, to reduce them to the status of things; and so he stresses subjectivity as against objectivity: human personality must keep its central place amidst a world of science and technology.

(e) His childish enthusiasm behind him, modern man has learned through some painful experiences to become a realist. The ideal secularized man is a dream which has yet to come true. His hallmark now is *self-criticism*. There are three calamities in particular that must be countered. One part of mankind is being ruined by an unbridled passion for more consumption: it is the plague of de-humanization. Another part of mankind suffers and dies in the struggle for bare existence: it is the plague of the Third World. For yet another part of mankind their whole life is a "conveyor belt", an endless succession of repeated actions; they are exploited, accept that and want nothing else: it is the plague of massification, of a "robot" society. This threefold slavery must be eliminated—but how?

When in the course of this century—especially in Protestant circles—people started to use the term "secularization" or "secularizing" as a cultural-cum-philosophical category intended to pinpoint what is distinctive about the socio-cultural changes taking place in the Western world, they were expressing in this one word all their dislike of modern culture: secularization is the finish of Christianity *and* culture. This particular critique, as intemperate as it is undiscriminating, still exists and has even spread to certain Roman Catholic circles. After all that it has to be said that the criticism is irrelevant with respect to the first four points above-mentioned; but it does bear, in a rough and ready way, on the fifth one. Modern culture *may* turn out to be the finish of Christianity and culture, but in itself it is no such thing. The criticism reflects both pessimism and a nostalgic longing for an assured past, which because it is past can never return. As history demonstrates, this sort of reaction on the Churches' part to change and development is no new thing. The Church would be failing, and would destroy itself, if as being the institution of Redemption it had no redemptive answer to give to the modern world and therefore simply rejected it. A theology which has concluded that the post-Christian era has dawned already relegates the Churches to the ghetto, the wilderness and the "folkloriste" reservation or just writes them off altogether. What would help the world is for the Churches to continue with frank self-criticism in dialogue with the self-criticism of the secularization experts.

Liturgical renewal will not easily thrive in a Church dominated by pessimism. Those on the inside, however—that is, those who still do in fact maintain the celebration of liturgy—experience in it the power which Christianity possesses and which for Christians is the source of their interior strength. The renewed liturgy does encounter the secularized world, because both—in their own way—display the same typical features, as noted above in the first four points, and because where the fifth point is concerned the liturgy not only has the answer but can also offer the Redemption, the needed Deliverance. It is a lengthy process of *metanoia*, of *"conversio"*, "the narrow way" of the Gospel. In the working out of the *"reformatio ecclesiae a capite usque ad pedes"* since Vatican II there is a large element of disillusion. No wonder, then, that the liturgical renewal is being described as an "illusion".

III. Desacralization

One reason for the Churches' resistance to secularization is the fact that the whole thing has gone hand in hand with desacralization. The question is whether there is any intrinsic connection between the two.

Because secularization has come about in a christianized world (North, West and East Europe, North America) it is indeed accompanied by a hostile attitude towards certain *concrete forms* of Christianity, certain historical accretions, which are or seem to be, in whole or in part, in contradiction to it. The same period has seen the Churches having to deal with a not insignificant number of theoreticians who examine religion and Christianity critically in the context of the data afforded by the modern sciences and then reach conclusions that conflict with various opinions expressed by this or that established school of theology. Eventually, new "life views", new ideologies, come along, lumped together under the general heading of "humanism", which in effect write off religion and Christianity. All these phenomena have been laid by the Churches at the door of secularization and put down to its intrinsic negative side under the vague term "desacralization". Because the word "sacral", with its many synonyms, has so many different meanings,[6] it may be useful to make a number of distinctions before offering a conclusion as to the link between secularization and desacralization.

1. *The sacral in its most general sense* may be defined as the relation which man discovers and experiences between the reality of the world as it is experimentally and rationally known and a mysterious reality which is perceived in the mundane realm and yet cannot be grasped or netted like the mundane aspect of things. In other words the sacral is the opening and the access of the world *in man* to the wholly other, the transcendent, the absolute, the divine; and the religions are the social, institutionalized forms through which it is apprehended in experience. In this context desacralization means the *rejection of religion as incompatible with man's autonomy in his world.*

We are bound to say that the assertion that in its essence secularization is that kind of desacralizing process is untenable. First of all, through his scientific and technological achievement in the world man has simply changed his posture and style of accomplishment within that world without affecting what might lie within the range of his experience outside or beyond it. Although secularization is essentially a-religious, a mode of living in the world *"etsi deus non daretur",*[7] it is not a view of life or a theory about life or an ideology to be compared with, or set over against,

[6] H. Fugier, *Recherches sur l'expression du sacré dans la langue latine*, Publications de la faculté des lettres de l'université de Strasbourg, 146 (Paris, 1963). We have here a close analysis of the meanings of *"sacré"* and its associated terms in ancient Roman culture. Data on the use of the same group of words in the Tridentine Roman missal may be found in M. Ellebracht, *Remarks on the vocabulary of the ancient orations in the Missale Romanum,* Latinitas Christianorum Primaeva, 18 (Nijmegen, 1963).

[7] See D. Bonhoeffer, *Letters and Papers from Prison* (Fontana, London, 1959), pp. 120 *et seq.*

others. This desacralization, therefore, is extra-secular or metaphysical. The denial of a reality beyond the world or—to put it concretely and positively—any avowal of atheism, the rejection of the possibility of a divine revelation, the reduction of Christ to a purely human person, is not a secular discovery, hypothesis or thesis. Because within the secularized world it is a demonstrable fact that innumerable people live without any religion or easily abandon their religion, writers label this phenomenon *secularism*. In so doing they acknowledge the distinction to be made here from secularization, whatever else may then be thought regarding the terminology itself.

After all, one can also make the opposite assertion: *secularization opens up a new prospect for religion and most assuredly for Christianity*. Secularized man is aware of his autonomy, his independence, his power; but whilst he knows this in terms of experimental science, time after time he feels also his limitation. Faced with this, he can arrive at a crucial decision: to burst the door open or to slam it tight shut. Out of his *faith in the mystery of the Incarnation* the Christian feels aware of the presence of "God in the world". For him the world as it is is not conceivable without Christ, so that being now emancipated *vis-à-vis* the world, he understands it from the Scriptures, from Christ, better than it understands itself. The man who gives his backing to secularization is not a seducer but a promoter of humanity. The Churches make themselves culpable if they persist in anathematizing this secularizing process instead of working with it and for it, so to speak, in Christ's name. The Church is not a dispensary for our celestial needs in a world left to itself or left to handle by itself the course of its own development. The active manifestation of the Church in the world is the progress of the paschal mystery, proceeding from Christ's birth as man, through work, suffering, cross and burial to resurrection. In virtue of this mystery the Church corrects man's inappeasable urge to exalt, divinize or demonize his own progress; and it protects him from the tendency to let himself and his activity be fruitlessly dissipated in pessimistic resignation and sceptical agnosticism. Instead of laying the blame for desacralization upon secularization, the Church must *in Christ* release the modern world from its limit, its confine, so breaking through to what is truly sacral, man's resurrection in Christ to an exalted plane of human existence and to the full stature of the perfect man, in praise and in profession of faith.

This is the task of liturgy; and of this the company of believers renews its understanding, when at its gathering together it undergoes a profound experience of its divine-human growth and progress in Christ and, rich in that experience, discovers in its secular growth and progress the doorway—and takes also the path—to the final completion of all things in Christ.

2. Besides the sacral in its most general sense, the term has many special meanings which are classified here rather artificially, on the basis of a linguistic exercise.

(a) *Holy—Unhallowing* (sanctus—desanctificatio). In the strict sense of the word only *persons* are holy: that is, those who, being pardoned by God, devote or consecrate themselves to God. When the word "holy" (= "saintly") is used of God—Father, Son, Christ, Jesus, Spirit—it signifies "the source of holiness (= saintliness)"; with the exception of "the Holy Ghost", this term is used sparingly—and as an adjective with "Christ" and "Jesus" only seldom. A Christian must, *ipso facto*, be a holy person, a saint. In antiquity people talked about the communion of saints; and one wonders why for a long time past this has not been the case. The desecration or unhallowing of holy (saintly) persons is said to be profanation, sacrilege. The unhallowing of persons who have been called "saint" merely by custom or for frivolous reasons is a healthy kind of purging, unmasking or "de-Byzantinization". Thus "de-sanctification" is beneficial in that it serves to purify the language; for excessive use of a word empties it of its meaning.

In the new liturgy an attempt to aim at greater austerity is surely good. The repeated addition of "holy" to "Father" in the new eucharistic prayers is not meeting with universal appreciation, even though Christ sometimes did this in his prayers to his Father: he himself taught *us* to pray "Our Father"; that "our" says more to human beings than does "holy".

(b) *Sacred—consecrated—Desecration* (sacrum—consecratio—desacratio). "Sacred" in the strict sense of the word are Christian *actions* or *procedures* intended for the sanctification or christianizing of man. They are the *sacraments and sacramentalia.*

Desecration (*desacratio*) of these is said to be profanation, sacrilege. Even things used in connection with sacramental and sanctifying actions can be described as sacred (sacred by association) in so far as they have been picked out and set aside for procedures of that sort. When desecration of sacred actions or things implies the denial of their *value(s) qua signs and symbols*, then not only in religion but in the secular world too we are up against a dehumanizing process, rationalism, a defect of culture. Even in the various schools of theology one finds a gravely defective valuation of symbolism, with the result that they get silted up in rationalism and in a logico-juridical dogmatism (the polemics and casuistry of formulas). If in the Church the sacramental and sanctifying actions, the signs and symbols, have come to be a dehumanized and therefore unchristian automaton-like affair, an impersonal mechanism, a *"Verdinglichung"* (concretization—valid application of *"forma"* to *"materia"*), what we have is a desecrating and secularizing of the Church, which then loses its credibility.[8] Baptizing, offering sacrifice, eating and drinking, evangelizing, consecrating, marrying and dying—these are the dynamic growing process of the mystical body of Christ in dedication and surrender, and not an outward ceremonial on those occasions when this or that individual is entered in the church registers. What is required is not "administration", not a serving out, of sacraments (as one might be served in a shop) but sacramental *celebrations* in which the whole gathered congregation is consciously and Christianly implicated. It is not the pseudo-sanctity, the hypocrisy, of statistics but the liturgy of a holy people that makes the Church a sign set up for the nations.[9]

(c) *Sacral—Desacralization* (artificial Latin). These words refer primarily to the *(de)-sacralizing of mundane things and secular activities*. As the expression of a pantheistic and purely immanent conception of deity and religion, man divinizes things, forces and certain actions in order to exorcize the superior power of nature and propitiate the unknown powers. It is not only in religions that this phenomenon occurs, but also in the world—and in the

[8] On the many different meanings attaching to the notion of "credibility" see W. Gössman, *Glaubwürdigkeit im Sprachgebrauch*; stilkritische und sprachdidaktische Untersuchungen (Munich, 1970).

[9] Cf. Isaiah 11. 12.

secularized world even on an increasing scale: an aura of sacrality attaches to nationalism, ideologies, science, technology, money, sport, mass media, sex, drugs, and so on. New idolatrous and diabolistic pseudo-religions are appearing, new myths and taboos, whilst traditional superstition, fortune-telling and magic are again in vogue. Sacrality exists also in the Church; and there it is made attractive for people by being covered with a veneer of Christianity and tolerated and even encouraged by ecclesiastical authorities. The popularity of this kind of sacrality is subsiding through the hypnotic attraction of what is sacral in the secular sphere. Traders in devotional goods are having a bad time.

The liturgical renewal is out to oppose sacral abuses and therefore encounters resistance even in unexpected quarters: the rows centred around the new liturgical kalendar are evidence of this. Radical desacralization is necessary in this area—and that includes the casting down of idols and of sanctuaries, however profitable they may be as a source of income. Those who believe that the superstition "permitted" in the Church is somehow efficacious in countering secular superstition are misleading us; for they are as much given to mass suggestion as is the "wicked world" itself and are manipulating a gullible lot of people who will soon see through the "ecclesiastical" fraud, if only because of the crafty nature of the secular one. Only a sound Christian faith, wholesomely and redemptively expressed and experienced in a truly pastoral liturgy, is going to form human and emancipated Christians in our secular world.

3. The *conclusion* to be drawn from the foregoing analysis is as follows. True sacrality is the *Opus Dei*: through Christ and with Christ and in Christ, the person "under grace" dedicates himself to God and to mankind; Christ is the doctrine governing his life (orthodoxy) and is also his life's way (orthopraxy) through the world towards the eschaton. It is at the centre of what is done in celebrations of the liturgy, where Christ is dynamically present and the life of the faithful becomes an expression and revelation of the Christ-mystery and of the real nature of the true Church, the peculiar character of which is to be at once human and divine, visible and filled with invisible realities, engrossed in its work and yet on pilgrimage—and all of this in such fashion that in the Church the human is held in subordination to the divine, the

visible to the invisible, action to contemplation, the present to the city that we seek, which is to come. Hence it is that day by day the liturgy builds up the members of the household into a holy temple in the Lord, into a dwelling-place of God in the Spirit, to the measure that befits the fullness of Christ.[10] Having its life in true sacrality, liturgy spontaneously and quietly and without any reserve desacralizes "everything else". A properly cleansed and disciplined liturgy frees us also from sacral hocus-pocus by calling persons and things clearly by their name, so that we know just what or whom we are talking about without hiding behind this or that alibi.

IV. Desecularization of Church and Liturgy

To the end of this analysis I would append a hypothesis which, put in brief and succinct terms, is meant to provoke reaction and to stimulate further study and investigation.

Whether in the past or at the present time, one notices in many religions—as also in the Roman Catholic Church—a dangerous kind of pursuit: they want to constitute an independent *world* of their own side by side with the ordinary world, they claim to be a higher *world*, into which man must transfer from the inferior world (a *"fuga mundi"*). Thus there are supposed to be two separate worlds: *the religious, sacral or Christian world and the profane or secular world*. It is a widespread conception, a popular opinion, which in practice is to be found among all sorts and conditions of men. The contention here is not that *Christianity* has declared itself to be a different world, but that a tendency of this sort does exist in *Churches*; nor is it being argued that this tendency has any basis in dogma, but that the Church lives and behaves as if it were destined to be a world in its own right. One may refer at this point to the mode of operation based on the model of the two sectors of man's existence in the historical evolution of Western culture, which we were discussing in the first part of this article. This kind of outlook operates with a slogan borrowed from Scripture: namely, that the kingdom of

[10] *Constitution on the Sacred Liturgy* of the Second Vatican Ecumenical Council, art. 2.

God is *in* the world and not *of* the world . . . is therefore (?) an independent world of its own.

Now when the desecularization of the Church is discussed in this context, the point is going to be made that as it is developing at present the Church will be more than ever obliged to eschew every tendency to set itself up as a sacral world over and against the world.

The Church is not a world in itself, whether one chooses to call it a sacral one or not. What then is it? It is and always will be a *mysterium* in the strict sense: Christ is true God, proceeding from the bosom of God the Father, and true man, incarnated *in* the world and thus *of* the world. Christians (the Church), like all people and like Christ, are *in* the world and *of* the world, and as the children of God, being pardoned, reborn and redeemed *by* and *in* Christ, are therefore *of* Christ. The world's oneness resides in the fact of creation: man with his world created by God *ad extra* and by Christ *ad intra*.

Were an autonomous sacral world to be made of Christianity, that would be enough to belie it; for the divine reality is not a "world" and the human reality is fundamentally integrated into the "secular world". A Christianity supposed to be a sacral world would not be sacral at all but a secularization of Christianity, a profanation and thus something self-destroying. *There is a single world, in which the secular dimension is autonomous and the Christian dimension is autonomous*; in the tension between these two the world finds its deepest meaning and purpose and realizes its last and final goal.

A liturgy belonging to a "Church-world" is not able to function in the secular world. History shows that even within the Church the liturgy has been felt to be a little world apart, outside the ordinary life of the Church. Now that it is escaping from its isolation in the Church and at the same time opening itself to the secular world, it is once more becoming a "foreign body" in a Church where the pretension still exists that it is itself *the* world. If the liturgical renewal becomes a compromise, then it will compromise itself in a Church where opposition to the "Church-world" mentality is growing, and will lose its credibility in the secular world, because it will not be living up to the expectations aroused. Since the renewal of the liturgy simply has to start in a serious crisis within the Church, it cannot on its own account free itself from the general aporia of the Church and the world; nor can it really get beyond an interim solution. The great thing about it is that it should carry on amid the barrage directed at it from all sides.

Although much in it may still be imperfect and though it may leave a great deal to be desired, one has to admit all the same that the renewed liturgy is *in*carnated in the modern world. Like so much yeast or leaven, it essays to permeate, to work its way into the world *horizontally*, as it were, and at the same time to raise it *vertically* to its Source, its Salvation, its Eschaton—in other words, to its God, Creator and Redeemer. The liturgy is meant to be no longer an island, a ghetto, an enclosure with boundary marks or an Iron Curtain or a Berlin wall, nor yet a tower of Babel rising *vertically* at a tiny point of the *horizontal* world, but rather *the horizontal-vertical sign of the cross*. The liturgy becomes a dynamic force, opening up an introvert world, showing up its limits and clearing them away, abolishing its narcissism—and this it does efficiently, because its dynamis, its motive energy, is Christ, God and Man, who not as some obscure power but as a person is humanly active and spiritually illumined in divine love.

The liturgical renewal has set about the business of doing away with the "little world all on its own". It has ceased to have its own language (even if the texts still have to be translated from church Latin), its own music (but is still anxious about rhythm or beat, even if Fra Angelico's angels do have tambourines); and it has not rubrics but a ceremonial (although the danger of rubricism in a new form is by no means allayed). In a positive and critical spirit it is taking on from the world and its culture what is true and good and beautiful (so far with a certain amount of anxiety and reservation). It is making a determined bid to bring into existence real communities; and it likes to find places of assembly where the congregation can feel at ease, venturing to make its way once again into private houses. What it desiderates is an active congregation in which everybody, male or female, fulfils his or her proper task.

So far as inward renewal is concerned, a lot on the positive side is generally known. The way is open for a contemporary proclamation of the Word, for a dynamic sacramental life (instead of the "ministration", doling out, of sacraments), for a vital prayer-life. That this leaves a lot of things still to be desired is only to be expected. In accordance with a Tridentine outlook the new liturgical books have been imposed from above, although the local Churches made their voice heard and have been allowed a certain amount of latitude. This policy could not be avoided and indeed is opportune. It was impossible to renew the liturgy through the normal channel, that is, from the bottom up; for after centuries of inactivity the local Churches were not equipped for that. The new liturgical books from Rome are necessary as a liturgical framework and source of inspiration. They should activate Christian creativity in the immense pluriformity of the Roman Catholic Church. For a transitional period the way followed must be rated the only possible realistic solution. But that is not the end of the matter: our liturgical life will no longer be uneventful, as it was before, but will go on developing in accordance with the needs and demands of the future. In the new liturgy the Holy Spirit is not imprisoned in a golden cage. As in the second chapter of Acts the Christians who have been filled with the Spirit leave the upper room and hold the liturgy out of doors, where people of every nation under heaven are gathered together: "and they began to speak in other tongues, as the Spirit gave them utterance".

Translated by Hubert Hoskins

Eugene H. Maly

The Interplay of World and Worship in the Scriptures

THE first part of this article will present an interpretation of the terminology used in the discussion of biblical secularity. The second part will deal with the basic character of biblical liturgy in the context of biblical secularity. The third part will examine the role of the biblical prophets in the interplay of world and worship. The final section will propose a few thoughts on the role of prophecy in contemporary worship.

I. Terminology

The word "secular" is popularly understood as referring to "this world", the world of created reality. Secular pursuits, for example, are those in which man, as man and as part of created reality, is engaged in his day-to-day existence. Recent thought, however, has probed more deeply and sees the secular also as an expression of autonomy, or the ability to operate within the framework of existing reality without outside manipulation. (The word "manipulation" is important here, as will be seen.) While certain social and cultural conditions may limit the full exercise of this autonomy, the drive of man is towards maximum self-determination. When that is achieved, man is fully secular.

The theist will necessarily understand this autonomy as relative, not absolute, since, by definition, he accepts the presence of transcendent reality as in some way involved in the whole fabric of created reality. Just how this is to be understood will be discussed shortly. But we must insist here that relative autonomy, in the theistic view, does not necessarily mean a limited or restricted autonomy.

The word "sacred" describes the relationship of the secular to the transcendent reality. In the biblical view the whole of created reality can be declared a *bonum* (Gen. 1. 31), because it has been effected by the transcendent God and permeated with his covenant love (cf. e.g., Ps. 136. 1–9). This, of course, does not preclude the presence of evil in the world, but this is the result, not of God's on-going creative activity, but of man's sin (Gen. 3 ff.). This continuing permeation of the secular with the saving presence of God from the very beginning of creation is extremely important for a proper understanding of biblical secularity. It means that there are not two orders with which we are concerned, a "natural" and a "supernatural"—a concept that leads to the notion of a periodically *intervening* God and thus to the supposition of a manipulation of the secular when the "natural" order is deficient—but one order, in which creation's autonomy is conceived of as operating always in a transcendent order of existence. In this view, then, man's "relative" autonomy is limited or diminished only to the extent that he rejects the divine saving presence. On the other hand, to the extent that he accepts and embraces that presence he achieves ever greater autonomy and self-realization. The supreme manifestation of this is had in Jesus of Nazareth, whose unique self-consciousness as an eschatological person involved the total embracing of his Father's will and, consequently, the pre-eminent self-realization in resurrected glory.

We cannot here go into a detailed explanation of the biblical evidence that supports this view of the secular-sacred. But a word must be said about the role that history plays in the biblical interpretation, since it affects what will be taken up in the following sections.

It is still commonly accepted by the scholars, whatever may be the differences in details, that for Israel the revelation of God was conceived of as having been first experienced in history, not in nature. "The Lord our God brought us out of the land of Egypt with a strong hand and an outstretched arm" is proposed as one of the earliest forms of Israel's creed; it clearly affirms the divine activity in history. This, as has been pointed out by a number of scholars, is in contrast with the pagan interpretation of divine activity which they associated primarily with the cyclic phenomena of nature. The primary identification of Yahweh with the historical, rather than with the natural phenomena, opened the door to an interpretation of all history and, ultimately, of all reality as permeated by the divine presence. This was, of course, only gradually recognized. But it would eventually preclude an interpretation such as is found in 1 Kings 20, where the Syrian officials explain their defeat at the hands of Israel as wrought by a god of the hills, who, they thought, would have no strength in the plain (vv. 23–8).

"Sacred", then, is a word that is co-terminous with "secular" inasmuch as it, too, describes all of created reality, but in its relation to the transcendent order. The word "sacral", the final term, is used to describe that particular area of created reality which is considered to be under some special aegis of the gods or invested with a particularly numinous character so that it lies totally outside the range of man's control. Such is the "holy mountain" that man can climb only with the divine permission or the primordial times in which the gods were conceived to have performed those actions that would ultimately affect creation and history.

The "sacral", of course, is radically opposed to the "secular" since it denies autonomy and self-realization in those areas where it is applied. And the process of secularization is properly the process of desacralization, or ridding any part of created reality of that numinous character that would exclude man's rightful activity and control. It is our contention that biblical religion has been radically desacralized, or secularized, from the beginning by reason of the conception of God discussed above. There do remain, however, vestiges of the sacral in the Bible; these might be described as the "debris" of the break-through from a mythical or sacral world-view to an historical world-view. A clear example is found in Job 38–41 where a number of the questions asked of the plaintiff presuppose a sacral interpretation of parts of creation (cf. e.g., 38. 16, 18–24). The presumption here is that Job must answer "no" to these questions and so be brought to a recognition of the transcendence of God himself. Modern man could answer "yes" to the same questions: the process of secularization has reduced the sphere of influence of the "sacral".

The "sacral" is also opposed to the "sacred" but for different reasons. While the "sacred" does affirm the presence of transcendence in created reality, it does not do so in a manipulatory manner, so that creation would suffer any diminution of its autonomy. On the contrary, as we have already pointed out, the presence of transcendence gives a new and higher dimension to creation's autonomy. Moreover, the concept of "sacred" is not restricted to specific areas of God's activity but is affirmed of the whole of created reality to the extent that it has not been affected by sin or evil. It is with these three terms, and especially with the first two, that we shall be dealing.

II. Israel's Liturgical Worship

Mowinckel defines cult or ritual worship as "the socially established and regulated holy acts and words in which the encounter and communion of the Deity with the congregation is established, developed and brought to its ultimate goal".[1] These "holy acts and words" have reference, of course, to the Deity in his relationship to the people or to creation in general. It is in the conception of this relationship and in the consequent celebration of it in the liturgy that distinguished Israel from the pagan neighbours. That relationship, as we have seen, was first conceived to have been established in history, in the historical encounter of Yahweh with the sons of Jacob.

Israel's liturgical worship, then, celebrated the historical encounter and, in celebrating it, renewed it. This has long been the conviction of scholars, who have contrasted this understanding of cult with that of the pagans. Thus, Weiser noted long ago the historicizing, within Israel, of the pagan nature feasts. Passover, for instance, already in Israel's oldest tradition-history has a thoroughly historical character, recalling the exodus from Egypt.[2] Even while these feasts may be derived from pagan practices, "...in Israel they were cut off from their ancient roots; they lost entirely their magical and mythological rationale".[3]

Thus, in the pagan ritual celebration, it was the sacral element

[1] S. Mowinckel, *The Psalms in Israel's Worship* (Oxford, 1962), vol. I, p. 15 (Offersang og Sangoffer, Oslo, 1951).

[2] A. Weiser, "Glaube und Geschichte im Alten Testament", in BWANT, 4 Folge, Heft 4 (1931), pp. 36–43.

[3] Y. Kaufmann, *The Religion of Israel* (London, 1961), p. 115.

that predominated. There was the attempt in ritual to escape the tension of an uncertain history and to attain security through some kind of absorption into the mythical times of the gods. For the pagans ritual worship established or renewed the sacral or mythological.

One specific illustration of the distinctive character of Israelite cult is the use of the verb *zakar* ("to remember") and the noun *zikkaron* ("remembrance"). It is generally agreed that these words, as used in Israel's liturgy, were conceived to have the power of bringing into the present the object remembered; it was not simply a case of mental recall. Even more significant, however, is that the object of this effective recalling in the cult were the *historical* acts of Yahweh, not mythical actions of pagan deities. Ever since the exodus from Egypt "... it has been a basic element in Israel's religion that Yahweh acts and manifests himself in the actual history of the people. He is the *God of history* no less than the God of creation. Hence it is especially the historical facts of salvation which are 'remembered', and thereby turned into new effectual reality by Yahweh's presence at the festival. All he formerly did, gave and secured, he does and gives and secures again when he 'appears' at his festival."[4]

Our major concern here has been simply to point out the role that history played in Israel's liturgical worship. The pagans attempted to escape history and the secular through an initiation into the sacral. Israel's understanding brought her more deeply into history. (Recently attention has been paid to the close relationship between liturgical and eschatological imagery, which would confirm this analysis, since eschatology presumes a prevenient history.[5]) Historicization through liturgy is, then, a secularizing or desacralizing process. It brings man into more immediate contact with created reality (the secular), but inasmuch as that reality has been permeated by God's saving presence (the sacred).

III. The Prophets and the Secular-Sacred

In a previous issue of *Concilium* B. Vawter gave a survey of

[4] Mowinckel, *op. cit.*, p. 19.
[5] Cf. W. C. Doty, "Identifying Eschatological Language", in *Continuum*, 7 (1970), p. 558.

recent literature on the biblical prophets. One of his observations was that modern scholars are now, for the most part, agreed in rejecting the older position that the prophets, especially those of the pre-exilic period, were opposed "in principle to a ritualistic system that had no roots in the authentic Yahwistic tradition".[6]

Significant insights into the relation between prophet and cult were provided by S. Mowinckel in the work already referred to. He refers to the "seer priest" who gave oracles in the ancient Israelite cult, answering questions for the faithful (Vol. II, pp. 53 f.). Though the priest's role was later more concerned with the cult and sacrifice and with the technical apparatus of oracles and the prophets formed looser "guilds", from which the classical prophets developed, "the boundary between priest and prophet was never an absolute one" (p. 55). There was a sharper distinction between the official cultic prophets and the classical prophets (p. 57). But even in this case we must not hastily conclude that the cultic prophets were necessarily "prisoners" of the system, as though their inspiration were essentially different from that of the other, "freer" prophets (p. 65). Such a conclusion may be suggested by the fact that their oracular answers tended to be "pro-institutional" in the sense that they ordinarily predicted victory for the people in times of stress. Mowinckel points out, however, that, for one thing, these men were more psychically attuned to the people and to their desire for the Lord's favour, while the classical or "reform" prophets operated primarily from an awareness of Yahweh's moral demands. More profoundly, we can see in the nature of the cult, which rested on the conviction of Yahweh's faithfulness to his covenant and on the renewal of that covenant at the festival, the basis for the cultic prophet's trust in his inspiration and in his consequent promise of Yahweh's merciful help (pp. 65 ff.).

It cannot be argued *a priori*, therefore, that the cultic prophets were unaware of the imperfections of the people or that they did not make moral demands on them (cf. Pss. 24. 3–6; 50). If they do not show the same "moral earnestness, the energy with which Hosea emphasizes the moral commandments as being the demands of a holy God" (p. 71), it can be attributed to the fact

[6] "Recent Literature on the Prophets", *Concilium* (Dec. 1965), p. 62 (American edn., vol. 10, p. 115).

that they understood the cult as effecting and preserving the righteousness of the community as a community, as God's people; "... they express what the congregation ought to be able to say when it is at its best; they do not presuppose a minimum, but a maximum level ..." (p. 67). Their task, precisely as cultic prophets, was to announce salvation, not judgment.

While there doubtless has been an over-reaction to the position of Wellhausen with its supposition of a clean and radical break between prophet and cult,[7] most commentators today argue from a nuanced stand. It was not the cult that was the primary concern of the classical prophets, either to approve or condemn, but the will of Yahweh. Moreover, we can say, with some reason, that a true interplay between world and worship was not only recognized by the prophets, both cultic and classical, but was given significant direction by their activities.

One indication of this is had in the emergence in Israel of prophecy itself. The corrupt practices of the Elide priesthood (cf. 1 Sam. 2. 12–17; 8. 3–5) is not unconnected with the prophetic activity of Samuel or with the appearance of the bands of ecstatic prophets. One of the more obvious effects of their activity was to bring the word of God into the everyday life of contemporary man, thus protecting it against a sacralizing ritualization in the shrines and sanctuaries. Concomitantly it had the effect of suggesting an identification of the secular with the sacred. "By their exercises the prophets of the societies impelled the presence of the spirit, thus they contributed to uphold the spirit of God and spread holiness throughout the land."[8]

Another likely effect was that the element of preaching took on greater importance in the Temple worship. Especially illustrative in this regard is the book of Deuteronomy, where God's word is addressed to the *qᵉhal Yahweh*, the liturgical assembly. While the book as we now have it is admittedly late, it incorporates older traditions and was greatly influenced by the activity of the prophets who sought out the liturgical celebrations to deliver their sermons (cf. Jer. 7. 1; Am. 7. 13).

It is the content of the prophetic preaching, particularly that of

[7] Cf. G. Fohrer, "Remarks on Modern Interpretation of the Prophets", *Jour. Bib. Lit.*, LXXX (1961), p. 318.

[8] J. Pedersen, *Israel, Its Life and Culture*, III–IV (London, 1940), p. 111.

the classical prophets, that emphasizes the introduction of the secular into the ambience of the cult. The well-known and highly charged complaint of Isaiah against the senseless multiplication of sacrifices and prayers (probably given on the occasion of a liturgical celebration) is climaxed with the admonition to "seek justice, correct oppression, defend the fatherless, plead for the widow" (Is. 1. 10–17). In his Temple address Jeremiah warns against a false confidence based on the presence of the Lord's house and exhorts the people rather to "truly execute justice one with another", not to "oppress the alien, the fatherless or the widow, or shed innocent blood in this place . . ." (Jer. 7. 5–6).

It would be a mistake, however, to see the prophets as social reformers in the modern sense. Rather, such reforms were conceived to be the effect of an inner conversion that would recognize the divine character of the secular reality. The sacred and the secular were never divorced in their minds. It is quite clear that for them the chief reason for Israel's failure to show a *proper* concern for the secular was apostasy from Yahweh.

Faithless Israel did indeed concern itself with the secular in a sense that would be familiar to modern, capitalistic man. It busied itself with storing up its bread and wine, its silver and gold, with commercial transactions that made possible the building of winter houses and summer houses, houses of ivory and great houses (Am. 3. 15). But it failed to recognize in all these the dimensions of Yahweh's dominion. By reducing that dominion to its cultic life, it had plundered the secular of its true meaning. ". . . she did not know that it was I who gave her the grain, the wine, and the oil, and who lavished upon her silver and gold . . ." (Hos. 2. 8). Therefore must Israel be stripped of all these goods that her nakedness might be revealed (Hos. 2. 9–10). Then could Yahweh allure her once again and make her call him "My husband" (Hos. 2. 14–16). And then "they shall return and dwell beneath my shadow, they shall flourish as a garden, they shall blossom as the vine . . ." (Hos. 14. 1–7). Conversion to Yahweh was not, for the prophets, an escape from the secular; it was the necessary basis for a true appreciation and use of the secular.

The political world was also the target of the prophets' concern. They remain unique in the ancient world in the boldness and consistency with which they called upon king and prince to relinquish the power struggle, to give themselves to justice and righteousness, to "do no wrong or violence to the alien, the fatherless, and the widow" (Jer. 22. 2–3). But again, they cannot be considered political activists. Their concern was not with politics as such, but with politics as embraced by the transcendent order of Yahweh's covenant love. It was a secular-sacred concern. A clear example is Isaiah's classic reply to Ahaz, "But if you will not stand by me [i.e., Yahweh], you will not stand at all" (Is. 7. 9).[9] The prophet counselled military inactivism in the face of the threat from the north. From a purely political standpoint the advice made no sense, as Ahaz realized. But Isaiah had enunciated a faith-principle that has remained fundamental to biblical religion. It is found in John's gospel as Jesus' remark that "... apart from me you can do nothing" (15. 5), and in Paul's letter to the Philippians as "I can do all things in him who strengthens me" (4. 13). Only by a recognition of and total surrender to the transcendent Lord can man discover the true dimensions of secular reality and his own autonomy in the control of it.

The faith-principle of Isaiah was an explicitation of a reality that lay at the heart of Israel's religion from the beginning. But the explicitation was necessary in order that the liturgical celebration be restored to its original purpose, that of "recalling" God's gracious action in history and eliciting man's response in a secular-sacred world. Cult in Israel had gradually become divorced from the secular and had taken on a sacral dimension. It was this that the prophets saw and expressed in their denunciations of the magical rites that were multiplied in the hill-top shrine and royal sanctuary alike.

IV. Prophecy and Contemporary Worship

In the translation of Israel's prophetic-cultic experience into the contemporary world there are certain elements that remain constant. Christian liturgy remains the celebration of God's saving actions in history, specifically in Jesus Christ. Prophecy, too, remains a charism of the Christian community, and one that takes on a variety of forms as it did in Israel. Two of these seem worthy of comment.

[9] Translation from the Jerusalem Bible.

There is, first of all, the prophetic role of the president of the Christian assembly. Like the true cult prophet of Israel he proclaims, above all, the good news of salvation wrought in Jesus Christ and effectively recalled in the Eucharist. As such, his message will be one of joy and of the ultimate victory of God's reign. To deprive the people of this assurance would be to empty Christian liturgy and Christian life of all transcendent meaning. "I came that they may have life, and have it abundantly" (John 10. 10). While this is a "hierarchical" form of prophecy, it need not be "pro-institutional" in a chauvinistic sense.

But the "hierarchical" prophet also has the task of relating the Eucharist, over which he presides, to the secular world, lest liturgy lose its historical dimension and become a ritual drama offering escape into a magical or sacral world. Like the cultic prophet of Psalm 82, he must remind the people that they must "give justice to the weak and the fatherless; maintain the right of the afflicted and the destitute. Rescue the weak and the needy; deliver them from the hand of the wicked" (vv. 3–4). It is in the liturgical celebration that these admonitions must be given, since such acts of justice and mercy are the proper response of man to God who graciously calls him in community.

There is also the "free" or "non-hierarchical" prophet, layman or cleric, whose task is to bring God's word into the marketplace of social and political man. Like the classical prophet of old, his primary concern will be God's moral will, now as expressed in the message of the Galilean. But the direct object of his activity will be the world *as* world, as still in need of recognizing the redemptive love that has transformed it and made it "sacred". Like Isaiah, Jeremiah and Ezekiel, the Christian prophet may engage in ritual actions that will dramatize the meaning of a redemptive message. But always the aim will be that "conversion" that transcends social reform and political activity while it embraces them.

"Hierarchical" prophet and "free" prophet must not be at odds, just as liturgy and the world cannot be at odds. Without the world (the "secular"), the liturgy becomes a "sacral" rite of escape. Without the liturgy, the world loses sight of its "sacred" dimension. A constant interplay between the two will alone give meaning to both.

Antoine Vergote

Symbolic Gestures and Actions in the Liturgy

EVERY gesture which is not the manipulation of tools can be called symbolic. A technical gesture follows a predetermined end: driving a car *so as to* get somewhere, eating or drinking *so as to* satisfy a need for nourishment, turning on a switch *so as to* have light... these gestures do not express, they perform. But giving a present, shaking hands, bowing the head, embracing—these are gestures that express an intention and achieve it at the same time. We call them symbolic by analogy with symbolic words and objects, because they unite a bodily attitude with an intended meaning. They become symbolic signs, and rational language will never attain the richness of their communication. In religion, as in intersubjective life or in a work of art, meaning cannot be dissociated from sign.

The fact is that the gesture makes no break between the human order of the senses and that of ideas. It unites man with the space world in which he operates. And it does not separate expression, communication and action; it is a concrete relationship established with others, and in this relationship it gives a meaning to the visible world.

To study the symbolic meaning of gestures thus involves many points of reference. And our contribution aims at showing how the liturgical gesture is the point of union between man, the world and God.

For this entails serious consequences for the liturgist. The liturgical gesture cannot be conceived according to the finalist concepts that have played too big a part in our theology of sacramental actions. It must respect the truth of the body as lived, which is the source of our symbolizing powers. Finally, we cannot legitimately separate it from the cultural significance of space-time. We have chosen to develop these three data rather than give a descriptive picture of symbolic gestures—as the reader can easily find that elsewhere.

I. The Liturgical Gesture is Expression and Action

We want to begin by thinking about the status and function of the liturgical gesture. The faithful often question themselves about the meaning of liturgical participation: is it not enough to have the faith? Why "express" it? We were accustomed to seeing "practice" as a duty, but the meaning of external and legalistic obligation is gradually disappearing. Moreover, the idea of a grace granted by "means" of a rite does not convince as much as it used to. This change of outlook is not necessarily to be deplored: a critical phase opens the way for a rediscovery of the rite as being significant and operative in itself, as it is faith that is actualized.

No one doubts that gesture is of the order of sign: it is expressive. Its bodily nature, however, differentiates it from language: it does not have the semiotic autonomy of the latter. The gesture is inherent to our carnal subjectivity, even if it directs us towards the world and towards others. But its subjective and corporeal character does not diminish it, rather it confers on it the unique power of being expressive in an immediate way. Language and gesture complement each other. Thus the liturgy wins through to the truth of its religious function only if it avails itself of the complementarity of religious gesture and language.

Because of its bodily nature, gesture is narrowly bound to action. A distinction is generally made between gestures that are purely expressive and those that express something while achieving it, the intention of an action.[1] In the liturgy a distinction could equally be made between sacramental gestures which perform an action on objects (water, bread . . .) and those which

[1] Cf. F. J. J. Buytendijk, *Attitudes et mouvements: Etude fonctionnelle du mouvement humain* (Paris-Bruges, 1957), pp. 285 *et seq*. ("Algemene theorie der menselijke houding en beweging", Universitaire bibliotheek voor Psychologie, Antwerp, 1948).

simply express our attitudes before God (genuflection, bowing the head, the gesture of the person praying. . .). To us this distinction is unimportant for in the liturgy every gesture, even those regarded as purely expressive, are in fact a way of behaving. To bow before God is in itself a religious action. And it is precisely there that the function of the liturgical gesture lies: it unifies sentiment and action. It expresses and achieves.

So the liturgical gesture reveals a very advanced kinship with language on the one side and with action on the other. And it is no mere chance if the close connection with man's two other registers comes about only in the gestures of encounter, such as those of love. We may be permitted to point out the highly significant expression (if somewhat devalued by use) "to *make* love": that is, to accomplish it by gestures that express it. Apart from the gestures that put it into effect, love does not exist. That is to say, the emotion tends to fulfil itself by gesture so as to become efficacious. But the words that precede and follow the gesture express it just as much, and without them the gesture would not attain its full expressive valency nor its efficacy assumed in the first person. Similarly faith is expressed and achieved in word and gesture, precisely because it, too, is encounter brought about with the Other who is God.

So the liturgical gesture and the religious language of celebration reveal the essential particularity they have in common: to be the sign that expresses and effectuates. This similarity allows us to be actively present at a liturgy in a foreign language, just as it provides the alternation of gesture without words, words without gesture, and moments when the two modes of expressive action coincide. A just evaluation of the liturgical gesture as expression and action of faith also extricates us from a false conceptualization of the sacraments and their efficacy, and frees troubled believers from the impression of "receiving" from the sacraments as from arbitrary means of grace cut off from their personal attitude of faith. We are not disputing the truth of the *ex opere operato* doctrine. But if this principle is understood outside all reference to the efficacy of religious language and symbolic gesture, we are in practice led to regard the sacraments as a magic ritualism. Faith is not just a "condition" for the efficacy of the sacraments; it is achieved in the gesture and the word which, by this fact, are operative in the relationship with God.[2]

Thus the liturgical gesture is faith in action. To say that it expresses faith is a misleading formulation. It suggests that faith is an inner state of the soul which projects itself in an external manifestation, much as one expresses emotions, such as joy or fear or hate, by movements of the face or the hands or in the whole bearing of the body. But in themselves emotions are not actions. They are a perception of the qualities of the world and of others, an inner commotion, and as such they dispose towards action. Faith, on the other hand, is a disposition towards God which is actualized only in expression. To express it is thus to effectuate it. So no faith exists that is not actualized in a rite that is indissolubly efficacious gesture and word.

Let us go back for a moment to the confusion that arises when we view liturgical gesture as an action that transforms the object (bread, oil . . .) by means of grace. If we observe liturgical praxis and read theological studies devoted to it, we sometimes get the impression that gesture is down-graded to the manipulation of sacramental "objects". It often seems that the main concern is to respect the validity of the sacraments: exactly the imposed words must be said and the prescribed materials "used". Theological formulations concerning "matter" and "form" are largely responsible for this down-grading of the gesture. The current disaffection for rites is the consequence. At a time when the plastic arts, the cinema, the theatre and the ballet express and achieve, intensely and in truth, the dimensions of human existence, a liturgy transformed into a technical action of grace cannot fail to arouse deep uneasiness: the action is no longer humanly true. The fascination of the Orthodox liturgy for certain people is understandable on account of the sacral mystery that impregnates its whole proceedings. And certain current tendencies aiming at making the liturgy more simply human derive no doubt as much from a search for truth as from a secularized theology. Those who interpret the Eucharist as the celebration of man's brotherhood are rediscovering the equivalency between the gestures, actions

[2] Cf. our study, "Dimensions anthropologiques de l'Eucharistie" in A. Vergote, A. Descamps, A. Houssiau, *l'Eucharistie, symbole et réalité* (Gembloux, 1970), pp. 7–56.

and intentions which they are seeking to put in motion. Does this not show that the theology of the sacraments has let the substance of the gesture be lost—even though it is the symbolic human support of supernatural action? When gesture has ceased to be a genuine human action, reference to grace and divine action takes on the meaning of a reality arbitrarily added from outside, from up there, to a non-significant human action. A defective anthropology of the gesture and the word empties theology of supernatural as much as human significance. Liturgical gestures are thus the relationship with God concretely effectuated. They constitute a system of symbols: a whole that expresses and effectuates the meaning of a life (assumed in the first person) with God. Walking towards the altar, the offertory, baptism are symbolic acts because these gestures both bear the mark of and achieve the meanings they show to the eye. As with every true symbol they do not depend on anything else, but by themselves they achieve a pact with the Other recognized as himself.

II. The Symbolizing Body

Without gesture, language loses its power of assuming our existence; but gesture deprived of language ceases to have its significance. Together they achieve the symbolic relation that constitutes religion and faith. We began by pointing out that gestures make up a system of symbols, and we drew attention to the kinship between gesture and language. Now we must show that gestures are symbolic because the body carries the power to condense into superdetermined signs the whole man in his lived relationship with God.

A true perception of the function of gesture and of the way it complements religious language will enable us to answer various questions and intelligently to assess various inquiries. Why must we always keep the same rites, such as baptism and the Eucharist? Are they so universal that Christ wanted them to be identical across the various cultures and epochs of civilization? On the other hand, if we acknowledge the function and value of the universal gesture, how do we regard a plurality of forms?

To answer these questions we would have to have a thorough

knowledge of the body, movement, the imaginary and the symbolic; and really to become an expert in the subject we would have to have a grounding in the phenomenology of the body, the psychology of bodily schematics, and researches into aesthetics which investigate the relations between body, space and time in different types of civilization. We may hope that in the future liturgists will listen still more to the lessons of anthropology—which tell us as much about rites as do pathological studies, if not more. It is not only by reassessing the ethical demands of the Christian faith that we overcome the dreaded rift between rite and life, but by assuming into the rite all that is human in civilization.

It should not be thought that a sense of rite has entirely disappeared, whatever be the occasional reservations concerning the rites of the Church. It is not without significance that films almost always show a wedding in the form of a religious "ceremony", nor should we judge this custom lightly as some musty residue of sociological Christianity! At that decisive moment, when life is lived in the relationship between two bodies, man wants to symbolize it. He sees a sacred dimension in it which enshrines it in a relationship far superior to any social or even sexual function. He feels that in depriving himself of the rite he is down-grading his sexuality to being no more than a function of pleasure or of social rationalism. The nostalgia for the rite felt by many non-believers derives from the perception common to all humanity that to be human is to symbolize life.[3] It is, moreover, impressive to note how the hippy movements favour symbolic rites and use them to express their sense of an existence freed from the reduction to the technical function. And does not the almost religious fervour aroused by modern ballet also stem from the same demand for ritual symbolization?

We are not trying to reduce Christian rite to the symbolic celebration of the essential dimensions of life: birth, initiation into adult society, sexual love, human brotherhood, illness and death;[4]

[3] A number of contemporary authors have stressed the dimension of symbolization. We may mention, among others: Cl. Lévi-Strauss, *Anthropologie structurale* (Paris, 1958); J. Lacan, *Ecrits* (Paris, 1966); E. Ortigues, *Discours et Symbole* (Paris, 1962).

[4] To avoid all misunderstanding, we would refer the reader to our study on the Eucharist mentioned above; there we explained what we meant

but we want to sketch out the setting and function of the ritual gesture: it is enshrined in corporeal existence which is a field wide open to symbolization. And is it not significant that all the sacraments (apart from holy orders which is in the service of sacramental rite) concern precisely the essential dimensions of our corporeal being?

The ritual gesture reveals and unfolds the intentions of the body as lived. It inserts itself into the space of the humanized world, concretely links the subject to the human community, and attaches it to the Other who is source and ultimate meaning of its existence. Language, of course, performs the same linking functions. But if language proposes to us the basic significants which enable existence to be symbolized and bound to the ultimate (which is what "religion" is), it operates symbolization only when, by means of the rite, it comes down into our concrete being, into our attitude which is the body as lived. Outside of the rite, symbolic language remains empty, as is the language of a schizophrenic who treats words as if they were real things. Words must be filled with the existential density of the body.

By its very structure the body is, at one and the same time, nature within us, interiority as lived, and the subjective intention open on to the world and others. Natural and cultural, subjective and intentional, interior and place of exchange, the body constitutes our concrete being. A faith which does not assume the body's intentional actions and effective resonance is a faith foreign to existence. But because the body is the setting for symbolization, the rite must assume it as it is effectively symbolized, that is to say in the forms expressive of its own culture. As unifying nature-in-man with culture, the body is the very setting for sacred mysteries. Indeed, following the two aspects that constitute it, the body refers man to the symbolic beyond. As nature-in-man, it is the dimension of the depth where we rejoin the source of existence. And as tensional vector which opens us to the distant, it directs us, in the deepest part of ourselves, towards the Ultimate of our desire.

By its very nature, the body provides the opening to the symbolization accomplished in the arts, in love and in religious

about the institutional dimension which partakes of the symbol as performed, and which Christ took up in the account of ecclesial faith.

rites.[5] This opening is at once natural and cultural, and for this reason universal and culturally diversified. Whence the permanence and universality of ritual gestures, and also their diversified forms.

Let us check the truth of this analysis by taking a look at the two basic Christian rites: baptism and the Eucharist. Immersion in water and emergence from it is a gesture rooted in the deepest imaginations of the body. Myths, dreams, cosmogeneses, diverse religious rites and even the eldorados of leisure bear witness to it: in bodily symbolism man envisages birth into life as emergence from water. But baptismal practice, weighed down by a theology of sin which has sucked everything from it, usually manages to down-grade the rite of water to purification by washing.[6]

The Eucharist is a more complex rite. In the elementary gesture of the meal it brings together food and earthly joys and being-with-others. On the human plane these three elements that make up the meal are already highly symbolic: they express and achieve the permanence of life as nourished by the gifts of the earth, the feast that is being celebrated, and the family gathered together in participation. In the religious sacrifice-offering, which carries the active presence of Christ, the gesture of the elevation binds the human to the divine by the symbolic articulation of the horizontal and vertical attitudes. All the symbolic references of our bodily presence in the world and in others thus contribute to make the Eucharist the insertion of Christ into our concrete being.

Diverse rites can surround the essential ritual gestures. As we shall see, the forms they take depend on the specific manner in which certain cultural environments live and interpret the space-time of the world. But the rites that surround the nodal gestures

[5] On the symbolic body cf. the studies by M. Merleau-Ponty, F. J. J. Buytendijk, A. de Waelhens, L. Binswanger, E. Strauss, H. van Lier, E. de Keyser . . .

[6] On the effects of the false interpretation to which baptism, as watched, may give rise, cf. A. Vergote, "Regard du psychologue sur le symbolisme liturgique", *La Maison-Dieu. Rev. past. Liturg.* (Paris, 1967), pp. 129–151. And G. Fournier, G. Dechambre, "Signification de gestes et d'objets pour des enfants et des adolescents, *La Maison Dieu. Rev. past. liturg.* (Paris, 1967), pp. 163–172.

must always show forth the latter with full significance. That is to say that the liturgist must soak himself in both their existential and Christian meaning. Otherwise he will unnecessarily burden the Christian rite with all sorts of secondary rites—meaningless for people living now. The history of the liturgy as of all religions shows us that the invasion of secondary rites, overlaying and obscuring the nodal rites, occurs at epochs when theology has cut itself off from living anthropology as well as from Christian sources. Uncertain as to the efficacy of its actions and indifferent to the human meaning of gestures, the liturgy then tends to back up its rites by accessory and meaningless gestures, perceived if not lived as a quasi-magic ritualism. Only think of the multiple duplications that used to overburden the Latin eucharistic rite several rites for the introit, the offertory and the blessing of the species.... Is it not significant that the faithful who, rightly, demanded a simplification of our eucharistic rite, at the same time admired the Orthodox rite which is so redundant? The point is that the latter is seen as an organic unfolding of the Christian mystery and of human culture. But we must also note that the Orthodox rite is conceived according to the symbolic norms of another cultural and religious area; the cultural diversity of peoples and epochs prevents us from adopting, just like that, a liturgical style that does not belong to us.

III. Cultural Diversity in Universal Symbolization

The more we become aware of the diversity of cultural forms, the more are we amazed by the incredible rationalistic naïvety of those who wanted to maintain and impose the same ritual forms throughout cultural time and space. They behaved as if gesture, song and prayer did not affect our subjective being; the believing man, by a sort of absolute bestriding of space and time, would in the same way be open to pure theological concepts!

We believe that the liturgy should be situated at the intersection of three axes of thought. As we have already suggested, the existential body is universally structured following symbolic dimensions that enable all men to meet in the same basic gestures (giving presents, immersion in water and emergence, bowing the head...). Secondly, Christian belief informs and transforms space-time as lived and directs its apperception in a specific way.[7] Thirdly, the evolution of civilization considerably modifies our own perception of space and objects.[8]

Because the ritual gesture is the body in action, it should take place within the space-time of a determined cultural environment, under pain of presenting itself as magic and outworn ritualism. The Orthodox rite of baptism can impress us by its recurrent gestures of anointing and immersion. But the story told us by a Catholic sociologist is instructive. He invited a Marxist friend, a member of the Academy of Sciences of Moscow (an unbeliever but without hostility to Christianity), to attend a baptism in a Russian church. The latter was disconcerted by so much ritualism, the redundancy and complexity of which left him with the impression of unbelievable magic. We, for our part, have often been told the same thing by unbelievers who attended our Requiem Masses in the past. Reduced to an expressive simplicity, would not these rites have been more eloquent through a native and direct symbolism? Experiments have proved it. However the Orthodox rites, in a specific cultural area, have had and still have their power of symbolic evocation.

The Greek temple and the dark cavern of the Eastern religions symbolize light in quite different ways, yet with both the relationship with the divinity is evoked, though in the two types of religion man is situated quite differently in relation to the world and the divine.[9] Similarly the Orthodox eucharistic rite is correctly celebrated only in the architectonic space of a Byzantine church which gives suitable form to its cultural and Christian apprehension of space-time.[10] The function of a Byzantine church is to be the architectural space wherein can be celebrated the light of the rising sun, symbol of the nativity and the resurrection. In this receptacle of light, where icons represent the procession of spiritual eternity across the ages, the ritual gestures of repeated processions, and of the covering-up and uncovering

[7] The reader will find this idea admirably expounded and illustrated in E. de Keyser, *Art et Mesure de l'espace* (Psychologie et sciences humaines) (Brussels, 1970). Cf. pp. 93 *et seq*., pp. 151 *et seq*.

[8] Cf. e.g., "Les Objets", *Communications 13* (Paris, 1969).

[9] Cf. R. Bultmann, "Zur Geschichte der Lichtsymbolik im Altertum", *Philolgus* (Berlin, 1948), pp. 1–36.

[10] G. Duthuit, *Le feu des signes* (Geneva, 1962), pp. 80–81.

of the sacred, take on their authentic Christian meaning and incarnate faith within a specific and cultural vision of space and light.

It would be against nature to transplant these rites into a stripped modern chapel, with walls of hard bare concrete and where the light is not distilled but omnipresent—as in the world open to technical objects. Similarly we cannot imagine an Eastern service in the church built near Mexico by the Marxist architect, Candela: a huge open shell closed behind the altar by an expanse of glass that overlooks the factories and dwellings of a workers' city. The same essential gestures of our liturgy can and should inspire scenic forms corresponding in an organic way with the multifarious forms of human existence.

It seems to us that the liturgy of today should operate along various lines, answering by its adapted styles to the diverse needs of contemporary man. The three main lines seem to us as follows:

A man's existence is divided between various sectors of which the two most essential are the family and the vast social and political community. He wants to preserve the intimacy of his family—all the more as urban society increases in multiformity and anonymity; but he also wants to open his family on to society where he desires to be actively present both as social man and as Christian. It is hence normal that contemporary man should discover the significance of a liturgy in small groups—of family and friends—and that he should also want to insert the liturgy within the social (e.g. professional) milieu, and it goes without saying that the liturgical style should be adapted to these two distinct functions. We celebrate differently when seated round a table (as at the time of the apostles!) from when we are gathered together in a factory, a stadium, or a parish church. If the celebrant's lay clothing suits a family living-room, it strikes a false note in a Gothic or Baroque church. We can well imagine a sacred dance in a cathedral or a stadium, but not in a Romanesque chapel. And does not the seated position throughout the whole of the eucharistic celebration take on a different meaning in a family group from in a vast edifice? Some liturgists who dream of nearness and family intimacy seem not to realize that at certain times man also wants to live the sacred mystery in the context of the universe. While others are so drawn to the Byzantine concept of the sacred that they cannot imagine a liturgy rooted in the simple day-to-day life of the family. We should bear in mind that liturgical celebration partakes of the festival that symbolizes the multiple dimensions of existence.

Contemporary Western civilization is strained to the utmost by its infinite variety of cultural styles as manifested in its museums, in its studies of history and aesthetics, in its travelling theatres and ballets. The multiplicity of inventions seeking a new style—after the destruction of all tradition—shows that contemporary man no longer imagines that one uniform space shall enshrine the relationships of his body with things. This is surely one reason why the most educated men are searching for ways to unite themselves in a return to stripped forms, those near to natural being. The style of the liturgy could be inspired by these many researches and—in order to respond to the various styles that expand contemporary sensibilities—it could give free play to the experiments worked out by various groups.

A third principle of liturgical style might seem at first glance to contradict what has just been said. For the rite, if it is to be a recognized language, demands a certain stability of form. And if it is to incarnate life it must adopt the law of recurrent gestures. Everything really near to life (meals, sex...) is cyclical in character and is practised in repetitive forms. So we would think it inopportune to be for ever imposing innovating experiments in the liturgy. The opposing requirements of repetition and creative invention, of uniformity and diversity, demand that the liturgy should offer diverse modes, following the rhythmic alternation that marks the shifting life and culture of contemporary Western people. In order to find the golden mean, in order to rescue the liturgy from both deadly repetition and inorganic explosion, the liturgists must have a deep psychological sensibility and be well-informed as to the styles of life of the various cultural groups.

It is in any case to be regretted that at the moment the simplification of the rite has often brought with it the suppression of elementary ritual gestures on the part of the faithful. An overconcern with their participation in song has brought about a neglect of their participation by various bodily attitudes expressing naturally the various moments of relationship with God: deep inclination, the standing or seated position, the procession (whether by delegation) towards the offerings, and so on.

Conclusion

Liturgical gestures are movements that express and achieve the various relationships of concrete man with his God. They have the power thus to express and achieve because the body as lived always carries a human meaning within it. To effectuate this meaning before God is thus to assume our humanity in a faith in action. To raise upwards the gifts we offer is to take in the whole horizontal dimension which defines being-in-the-world, and to join it with the Other who is its source and ultimate meaning.

Because the body as lived is always intentional and hence symbolic, its gestures constitute a system of symbols related to language. Emergence from water as entry into the new life is accomplished once only. But the sacrificial and communal meal represents an act as recurrent as life which physically feeds on and enjoys the riches of the earth.

To say that liturgical gestures are a system of symbols implies also that they achieve of themselves life with God. They *are* life with God, the action of faith that is accomplished. They have no finality outside that which they achieve. And to ordain a finality for them is to destroy their symbolic efficacy.

By reason of their symbolic insertion into space-time, the elementary and universally symbolic gestures that make up the core of the liturgy are surrounded by expressive gestures which should be incarnated in the real space-time of the concrete human environment. Thus the liturgy should allow of freedom for forms culturally and socially adapted. If not, the nodal gestures of the rite will not assume the really human within faith in action.

Translated by Barbara Wall

Eugene C. Kennedy

The Contribution of Religious Ritual to Psychological Balance

MAN is a maker of rituals; he strives to put a shape on his more valued experiences in order to keep them in the focus of his consciousness, prizing them as sources of strength and direction for his life. Men are always trying to write the best of their lives, especially the best of their lives with each other, into some kind of shorthand of word and gesture. Traced first on the walls of his cave and danced around campfires, this symbolism also shows up in poetry and painting, in world's fairs and family reunions, in handshakes and embraces. It is second nature for man to develop properly expressive rites to underscore the things that are most important to him: the beginning and endings of life, the celebrations and the sadnesses, the deep but sometimes fleeting moments of trying to reach beyond himself. Take away man's rituals and you render him vulnerable again to the terrors of a universe that has slipped out of the control of his understanding. Man makes the world familiar and life in it negotiable through ceremonial.

Religious ritual has a long history but it has always been very close to man. Coloured by the cultural periods through which it has passed, religious ritual has worn the masks of a thousand nameless gods. Religious observance for the Christian is now meant to express the whole range of human experience that is touched and illumined by the Spirit. Religious formulations have served man well, catching in a phrase or a movement what he can hardly express for himself, putting into word and symbol what he can recognize as his own yearning for the life of the Spirit. Healthy religious ritual contributes to psychological balance when it helps to redeem man as he struggles to find himself in relationship to God and to others. At its best ritual is deeply sensitive to the human stirrings of growth and human tendencies to weakness and makes room for both in its patterns. Ritual becomes a source of affirmation for a man who gives himself wholeheartedly to the resurrected life; it reaffirms him when his hope is frayed or when his humanity is all too evident to him. Ritual that springs from a pastoral orientation to fallible man makes him aware of the forgiveness that is available, the forgiveness which he can experience more fully when it is adequately symbolized to him. Religious ritual, in other words, promotes psychological balance when it matches man's efforts to fulfil his own deepest aspirations for growth, for redemption, and for fuller relationships to others.

Religious ritual, however, can also be used to entrap man and to manipulate him so that he does not recognize himself or come to a better understanding of his real destiny. Ritual which should free people for the life of the Spirit can be used as a source of control as well. Rhythmic repetitions of certain formulas lull the consciousness of the individual, conferring on him the deceptive kind of peace that is really passivity. This technique goes far back in history and every religion has seen its use at one time or another. This makes something less of man rather than something more. It is a pacifying ritual that robs man of the initiative he needs to respond to the Spirit and makes him an easy prey for those who would control him. We have not fully emerged from the era of bread and circuses in which great colourful gatherings relieved the drabness of everyday life but also cleverly manipulated the people's loyalties at a sub-intellectual level. The well-conducted rite supervised by the wrong leader can still turn a community into a mob ready to do his bidding.

Rituals have taken on a compulsive character at times so that they express neurotic conflict rather than healthy religious feeling. This was the kind of obsessive ritual observed by Freud, who shrewdly observed the enormous feeling that was transferred into the endlessly repeated religious formulas. Their real significance lay in the fact that they symbolized something unhealthy about the individuals who performed them. This style of ritual can be recognized because of the sense of restraint that dominates its repetitions. It is only if the person who performs the ritual is interrupted that we get a glimpse of the deep and often quite conflicted feelings that are being expressed through this behaviour. This style of ritualistic behaviour does, in fact, help the person who uses it to maintain some kind of balance. It is at a high price, however, because the relief of pressure comes only through the person's enslavement to a certain pattern of prayer or behaviour which is insistent and unyielding in its grip on the individual's psyche.

At other times, religious ritual is given a bad name because it is rooted in the somewhat distorted needs of the celebrant. It is no secret that certain aspects of religious services attract the maladjusted. The Church is no stranger to the minister who worships himself rather than God. When neurotics use these ceremonies to satisfy their own psychological yearnings they can hardly be the developers of ritual which can contribute to the psychological balance of anyone else. They drain off quite narcissistically the energies of the ritual, letting it revolve around themselves more than anything else. It is not unusual to find persons of uncertain psychological maturity deeply interested in the liturgy precisely because it offers them such an opportunity to make themselves the centre of all eyes, the arbiter of a ritual which has a private meaning and frequently unconscious for them. This neurotic orientation separates them from the community which they are supposed to be leading in worship. These people are performers, bathing in the limelight, isolated in their masturbatory use of ritual for their own needs. It has been a long and difficult job to rescue religious ritual from the hands of those who, all unconsciously, have used it in this fashion.

Ritual that contributes successfully to the psychological balance of persons must be rooted in a healthy view of man. It is characteristic of misdirected or immature ritual that it presents us with a distorted view of man. Ritual will never serve mankind well until our celebrations and memorials are built on a clear Christian concept of the way human beings actually live. Endless rituals have been produced which are true to some theoretical liturgy but false to life itself.

The rites of the Church must, first of all, recognize and ratify man as a psychosomatic unity. He is mind and body, intellect and emotions, all operating in relationship to one another in a quite extraordinary and integrated fashion. Ceremonials which fail to recognize man's unity chip away at his sense of personal identity. They tend to confuse and fragment his understanding of himself, making him feel lost and unsure at the very moment when he should experience his personal unity in a profound way. Prayers and rituals that are based on the notion of a divided man, man the pure spirit hampered by a body pulsing with libido, are counterfeit and cannot possibly contribute to the psychological balance of the worshippers. These distort man, taking him out of relationship to himself and therefore distorting his relationship to God and making it more difficult for him to open himself to the Spirit. Ritual that comprehends man's unity contributes to his dignity and to the successful achievement of his personal identity. It builds on and reinforces the growth processes that are the basis of the life of the Spirit.

A further characteristic of a healthy person is that he is constantly growing. Health is not a static condition, a moment of life frozen for ever like a photograph. Man moves always on, finding new challenges as well as new opportunities. He confronts unexpected crises but he also discovers unexpected strength and new dimensions of his personality. Ritual that does not leave room for man to grow frustrates him because he will be too confined and stifled to respond to the Spirit. This kind of ritual harvests the classic symptoms of frustration: apathy, restlessness and sometimes aggression.

Man is continually surprising, even to those who have spent a lifetime in studying him. It is impossible to chart all the characteristics of healthy men. In the long run the best test of any religious ritual is whether it finds a resonation in the healthy Christian. The mature Christian will react clearly to ritual that symbolizes his experience well. He will recognize the Spirit in it. The makers of ritual have all too often approached man from the outside seeking to form him according to some notions of their own. It would be better to approach men who are open to the Spirit and learn from them the kind of creative and spontaneous expressions of belief that are psychologically balanced. These rituals can then become the basis for a pattern of ceremony that is human enough to bear the weight of man's worshipping.

Putting man the worshipper at the centre of our concern enables the development of forms that enable him fully and flexibly to express himself in the presence of God.

These are incidental aspects of man which we should remember when we try to shape his religious rituals. Man is, quite fortuitously, distractible. He is made that way, constantly searching his inner and outer environment for new stimuli. Were this not so, man would never notice danger, or have a new way of looking at something; he would never be original or creative and his dreams would be dull. Failure to acknowledge this deep characteristic of human beings can only make them feel guilty when they cannot hold their attention completely and continuously on some religious act. Distractibility is one of man's strengths and part of his charm. It can hardly be treated as something man has to do away with if he is going to worship the God who made him the way he is.

Man is also serendipitous, that is, he is always finding things that he is not looking for. This is precisely one of the things that he can do in ritual that is developed with a healthy sense of what humanity is like. People may be struck at this moment by one aspect of the ritual, while tomorrow they may respond to some other part of it. Man abandons rituals that fail to make room for his distractibility or that are so impoverished that he can never find anything new in them. When they are not divorced from their tradition rituals present a pattern rich with the kind of associations that enlarge a man's sense of relationship with all Christian experience. In any case, religious needs in human beings are deep and it takes a great deal of human understanding to sense and express them with a ritual that will make man feel at home both with himself and with God.

Religious ritual must be basically respectful of man, enhancing his dignity, promoting his growth, and leaving him room for being fully human in the midst of his worship. Rituals cannot be used to control and manipulate or they will harm man quite seriously. Effective ritual can only be drawn out of man's life experience, sensed as present in the gestures and words to which man turns in his deepest moments of feeling. For this reason ritual must capitalize on the words and the style of ceremonies that men have found to be most expressive of their deepest values. We live, unfortunately, in an age in which the symbols of man's richest experience have been cheapened by those who have used them freely but without any feeling for the depths of human value they are meant to express. This is an awkward age of instant intimacy where amateur psychotherapists have tried to collapse human experience into weekends or even a few hours of confrontation in the name of communication. While there are many valid examples of group therapeutic effort, there are also very many confused prophets who speak the great ritual words of civilization in a shallow and superficial way. These people can only deceive men who seek to find and express themselves in the rituals of Christian worship.

The words we use have a long history. Words like *love*, *trust*, *openness*, *truth* and *community* are very close to the heart of the human race. A lot of meaning has gotten into these words over the centuries. When men use these words cheaply they debase them and they do a disservice to man's inherent dignity. As Gabriel Marcel has put it, "Our world is more and more given over to the power of words, and of words that have been in a great measure emptied of their authentic content.... It is hard to resist the impression that just because the realities for which these words stand are dwindling away, the words themselves are suffering an inflation, which is just like the inflation of money when goods are scarce."

Effective ritual demands maturity. It cannot be devised by those who have taken a quick look at life, made a grab for some of its treasures, and turned away again. These people corrupt ritual because they do not bring any fullness of life to it. They stand outside of it, demanding that it produce wondrous but sentimental experiences; all they reveal is their own immaturity.

Ritual that is based on man as he is opens him further to his own experience and to the experiences of other persons. It helps him, in other words, to deepen his Christian relationships; it makes it easier for him to be touched and enlarged by the Spirit. Healthy Christian ritual frees man to find the fullness of his response to the Godhead. When it is rooted in what is real about man and his authentic human experience ritual becomes the sensitive symbolic vehicle through which man can continually renew and reintegrate himself at every step in his journey through life.

Andrew Greeley

Religious Symbolism, Liturgy and Community

RELIGION, as Clifford Geertz has said, is "the struggle for the real". It is rooted in the "insufficiency ... of common sense as a total orientation towards life, but also must be viewed in terms of its formative impact upon common sense, the way in which, by questioning the unquestionable, it shapes our apprehension of the quotian world of 'what there is' and which, whatever different drummers we may or may not hear, we are all obliged to live".[1]

Religion, then, is a means of understanding ultimate reality; by answering the most basic questions that a man can ask, it provides him with an interpretation which will shape even the perspectives in which he views his daily life.

Common sense is not enough to explain life; the fact that life overflows the categories of practical reason is at the root of what Max Weber has called "the problem of meaning". It is most familiar in the West in the form of the problem of evil: why do the just suffer and the unjust prosper? "But it has many more dimensions, for the events through which we live are for ever outrunning the power of our ordinary, everyday, moral, emotional and intellectual concepts to construe them, leaving us, as a Javanese image has put it, like a water buffalo listening to an orchestra."[2]

Geertz insists that even in primitive societies religious belief coexists with scepticism. "There is a great deal of scepticism ...

[1] Clifford Geertz, *Islam Observed* (New Haven, Conn., 1969), p. 95.
[2] *Ibid.*, p. 101.

in traditional societies. The inevitable tension which remains between the deliverances of common sense and even the most compelling and comprehensive religion assures that, as does the widespread employment of religiously based power to less than elevated ends."[3]

If in the traditional societies scepticism persists, so even in the most modern societies, in Geertz's viewpoint, the religious perspective persists. At the heart of this perspective is "not the fearing that beyond the visible world there lies an invisible one (though most religious men have indeed held with differing degrees of sophistication to some such theory); not the doctrine that a divine presence broods over the world (though in an extraordinary variety of forms from animism to monotheism that, too, has been a rather popular idea); not even the more diffident opinion that there are things in heaven and earth undreamed of in our philosophies. Rather, it is the conviction that the values one holds are grounded in the inherent structure of reality, that between the way one ought to live and the way things really are there is an unbreakable interconnection. What sacred symbols do for those to whom they are sacred is to formulate the image of the world's construction and to programme for human conduct. . . .".[4]

The sacred symbol, then, represents a conviction about the inherent structure of reality. It explains that reality to us and tells us how we ought to live so as to be at harmony with reality. Whether the symbols be a credal proposition, a religious organization or liturgical ritual "(a people's) world view is their picture of the way things, in sheer actuality, are, a concept of nature, of self, of society. It contains their most comprehensive ideas of order. Religious belief and ritual confront and mutually confirm one another; the ethos is made intellectually reasonable by being shown to represent a way of life implied by the actual state of affairs which the world view describes. The world view is made emotionally acceptable by being presented as an image of an actual state of affairs of which such a way of life is an authentic expression."[5]

[3] *Ibid.*, p. 101. [4] *Ibid.*, p. 97.

[5] Clifford Geertz, "Ethos, World View and the Analysis of Sacred Symbols", *Antioch Review* (December, 1957), p. 422.

A religion, then, is as good as its symbols. "The force of a religion in supporting social values rests then on the ability of its symbols to formulate a world view in which those values as well as the forces opposing their realization are fundamental ingredients."[6] Man is a "symbolizing, conceptualizing meaning-seeking animal", and religion is his attempt to symbolize the ultimate reality. A religion will be effective precisely to the extent that its symbols are effective.

But one does not acquire one's "interpretive scheme" in a vacuum. One learns what the religious symbols are and what they mean from the society of which one is a part. One's meaning system is inevitably communal, both because one learns it from a community, and because it provides an ultimate base for community ties. We feel most at ease with, and most loyal to those people who share the same symbols we do, whose world view and ethos are the same as ours.

However relaxed we may be in the modern world with those who do not share our symbols of the ultimate, we are hindered in having authentic intimacy with them because they view the "really real" differently than we do. Religion is rooted in community; it reinforces community. Men believe as members of a society and then create their societies, or, more precisely, re-create them around their common beliefs.

Rituals are perhaps the most important of religious symbols because they appeal not merely to the human intellect but to the whole person. The enactment of a religious ritual calls upon the mind, the body, the emotions. In archaic societies it was the ritual itself that not merely expressed the content of the tribe's faith in the "really real", but also actually made the "really real" present among the tribe. The great mythological events of the past—as Mercea Eliade points out—became present in the ritual to be continued then by the tribe as it engaged in planting, cultivating and harvesting. The ritually enacted myth stood as a link between the mythological events of the past and the activities of the tribe in the present, the link which contained both the mythological event and the life of the tribe.

Edward Shils observes, quoting Durkheim, that ritual is a response to the *"serieuse"* in man, and he comments, "This I

[6] *Ibid.*, p. 426.

regard as given in the constitution of man in the same way that cognitive powers or locomotive powers are given. Like those, they are unevenly given and unevenly cultivated, so that the sense of the *'serieuse'*, the need for contact with the charismatic or sacred values, differs markedly among human beings within any society. Some persons, a minority, tend to have it to a pronounced degree and even relatively continuously; others, far more numerous, will experience it only intermittently and, except rarely, without great intensity. Finally, there is a minority which is utterly opaque to the *'serieuse'*."[7]

Nor does Shils believe that symbolisms of the world religions have been replaced in contemporary society. "The need for order and for meaning in order to allow itself to be bereft of the rich human race as a whole to allow itself to be bereft of the rich and elaborate scheme of metaphorical interpretation of existence which is made available by the great world religions. The spread of education and scientific knowledge, as well as the improved level of material well-being, will not eradicate them unless those who have these religions in their charge lose their self-confidence because of the distrust the highly educated hold towards the inherited metaphors."[8]

Geertz, Eliade and Shils, then, view religious symbols and religious rituals as necessarily rooted in man's need for an ultimate explanation of reality to which he can commit his total person, and of a moral ethos rooted in that reality which will regulate the activities of his life. All three authors would agree that there is little possibility of religion or religious symbols vanishing from the world; Geertz and Shils both add the remark that even in the so-called archaic societies of ages of faith, the importance of religious symbols varied from person to person. The sceptic, the agnostic, the hypocrite are not necessarily more prevalent today than they were in the past. "Spiritual responsiveness varied then as it varies now, probably just as widely. There was a gap between social ideas and social practice as there is now, probably just as broad."[9]

One would note in passing that this sophisticated view of the

[7] Edward Shils, "Ritual in Crisis", *The Religious Situation*, Donald R. Cutler, ed. (Boston, 1968), p. 747.

[8] *Ibid.*, p. 748.

[9] Geertz, *Islam Observed*, p. 114.

role of the sacred ritual in human life as described by anthropologists and historians of religions and sociologists is quite different from the rather naïve "secularization" model embraced by so many theologians—not infrequently even in the pages of this most responsible and respected journal. I must confess I frequently find it paradoxical that admitted non-believers, such as Geertz and Shils, argue persuasively for the survival of the sacred symbol and the ritual in the modern world while Christian theologians seem to be not only willing but even eager to report an absence of the sacred. My conviction is that they have not looked hard enough for it and perhaps don't even know how to.

This lengthy introduction on the nature of the sacred symbol, and its place in the contemporary world, is essential if we are to say something about the symbolism of Christian liturgy and its dependence on Christian community. Liturgy is not merely something we do either out of devotion or to honour obligations. It is a ritual enactment of our belief and contains within itself a symbolic "interpretive scheme". The liturgy brings us into contact with the "really real", not merely because God is somehow present among us in the liturgy, but also because an explanation of reality and a normative order for human conduct are summarized in the liturgical ritual. If the liturgy is to be a sacred symbol at all, it must contain within itself in a clear and impressive way both the world view and the ethos of Christianity. To the extent that it fails to do this, it is an ineffective symbol. The *"sacramentum"* which does not reveal that which it was designed to reveal is a poor *"sacramentum"*.

Those who are concerned then about the role of liturgy in the life of the Church must ask themselves above all else the critical questions: Does the initiate who experiences the Catholic liturgy have a sensation that his total person has been "seized" by the world view and the ethos which constitute the core of the Christian concept of the Real? Does he have a powerful and pervasive feeling that he has been in contact with that which is at the very centre of his faith? If he does not, then the enactment of the ritual is deficient. One presumes from having read the Constitution on the Sacred Liturgy that the liturgical reforms of the past decade have been designed to make the world view and ethos of Christianity overwhelmingly obvious to those who celebrate the liturgy. One has the impression that thus far the attempt has not been notably successful.

The Christian Eucharist, like all religious rituals, is obviously communal both in that it is by a community and in that the members of the community learn it precisely enacted in so far as they are members of the community. But something much more important than this must be said. The Christian liturgy is a special kind of symbol precisely because it wishes to say something special about the nature of human relationships. It is a meal; indeed, a meal which is both a ratification and reinforcement of intense and intimate human love. Modelled, as it is, on the Jewish Passover, it is a *family* event and emphasizes both the intensity and the intimacy of the family relationship. We would have been forced to conclude, I think, that the Christian liturgy attempts to provide a world view and an ethos through a ritual enactment of a family love even if we did not have the fifteenth, sixteenth and seventeenth chapters of the Gospel according to St John, but that touching and powerful account of the intense intimacy Jesus felt for his followers can leave no doubt in our mind that the Christian world view and ethos are memorialized in a love feast.

Given the pervasive sexual imagery of both the Old and the New Testament, one can, without any exaggeration, say that the love feast is a wedding banquet. The Christian liturgy celebrates the intense intimacy of the love of Christ for his spouse, the Church. The sexual union between married lovers is to be the model of the love relationship among Christians; the passion, tenderness, concern, challenge, responsiveness, affection which mark a union between a husband and wife who deeply love one another, and whose love spreads out to embrace their family and the rest of the world—this union is to be the model for relationships among all Christians.

One can only assert that the symbolism of the Christian liturgy is imaginative and daring. One can almost say that it is revolutionary; the Christian liturgy says that the "really real" is love—tender, passionate, intense, dedicated love. Its world view is the concept that God loves man even more intensely than a husband loves his wife; its ethos demands that we all love one another even as God has loved us, and as Christ, God's primary manifestation among us, has loved us. One can only repeat the words of G. K. Chesterton, "It is not that Christianity has been tried and found wanting, but found hard and not tried."

But in the face of this daring and revolutionary symbol, the sociologist is forced to observe that the symbol loses much if not all its impact in a large congregation of strangers or even of mere acquaintances. To put the matter bluntly, Christian liturgy, as it is now celebrated, is not a family meal, a love feast, a wedding banquet or, even for that matter in most instances, a celebration (and, as the Reverend Gerard Broccolo pointed out in an earlier issue of *Concilium*, most of those who are supposed to be celebrants are not very "celebrating" personalities). On the contrary, if the Christian liturgy, as it is celebrated in most parishes, resembles anything in the way of a meal, it is a cafeteria in which people eat their meals as isolated individuals, not only without intense relationships, but without relationships of any sort.

At the time of the promulgation of the Constitution on the Sacred Liturgy, a number of sociologists commented that it was unfortunate that those who framed the Constitution did not have more sociological and psychological *peritti* available for consultation. Social scientists would have pointed out that however splendid the vision of that Constitution, it did not devote itself to the practical questions of personality, society and organization which had to be faced if Christian liturgy was once again to become an effective symbol to those who participate in it. I was forced to say at that time that I very much doubted that the reforms envisaged in the Constitution would have much impact on the revitalization of the symbolic contact of the liturgy. None of the reforms that have taken place since has, I think, come to grips with this problem. Surely, the liturgy is a far more impressive and meaningful *ceremonial* than it was in 1960; but, as an emotionally pervasive symbolization of the intense and intimate love which is at the core of the Christian conviction about the "real", the Roman liturgy is still pathetically inadequate. Nor will it even begin to become adequate until far more serious concern is given to the crucial question of the large Sunday congregation. I do not know how you can have a family banquet or a love feast with five hundred or a thousand people.

The rise of the "household ministry" or the "underground church" (as described by Father McBrien in a recent issue of *Concilium*) or, to use my own phrase, the "new community", is a result of the failure of the official liturgy to cope with its own symbolic inadequacies. The underground liturgy is a creation of those who want in their liturgical experience more of what liturgical symbolism was originally designed to convey—that is, intimate and intense friendship. They argue that when Jesus said, "By this shall all men know you are my disciples that you love one another", he meant just that; and they conclude that a liturgy which does not ratify and reinforce intense friendship among the members of a Christian community is a liturgy that is seriously inadequate as a symbol. Whatever abuses may have crept into underground communities—and I am sure there are many—it seems to me that their basic position is unanswerable. Despite the occasional madness of the underground (marijuana mass, mass with crackers and whisky used as the elements for consecration, "teen-age" masses with Coca Cola and hot dog buns), it still must be said that the underground is a judgment on us for our failure to understand the implications of the symbolism of the Eucharist as a family meal. If we do not provide a family meal for an increasing number of Catholics, then they will provide one for themselves.

A frequent conclusion to the line of reasoning that I am following in this article is a demand that large parishes be abolished. Whether such demand is practical or not seems to me to be questionable. However, a more moderate recommendation —and one that labours under the handicap in our time of romantic pronouncements and little action that it could be easily implemented—is the suggestion that within the large parishes, more and more attempts be made to multiply the number of small liturgies. The Sunday liturgy, then, in the parish church involving large numbers of people would not be a banquet of isolated individuals but a banquet of communities, a banquet in which a number of "families" have gathered together with other families to celebrate their unity in a large community.

Some theologians have argued that it is the role of liturgy to "create community" but such an argument seems to me to be quite naïve. Symbols do not create communities; they rather ratify and reinforce communities which already exist. The intelligent parish priest does not try to impose his own predesigned liturgical communities on his people. He rather finds the natural communities within his parish and permits these communities to celebrate and deepen their unity through the liturgical ritual. The theologians who argue that liturgy ought to create community overlook the extremely important fact that a symbol is not a symbol until it is already shared by a community. A symbol does not create the act of sharing; it rather flows from the sharing.

The word "community" is used frequently in contemporary Catholic discussion, generally without it being clearly specified what the word means. However, the "sociologist community" has a very definite and specific meaning, perhaps best expressed by Robert Nisbet:

> By community I mean something that goes far beyond mere local community. The word, as we find it in much nineteenth- and twentieth-century thought encompasses all forms of relationship which are characterized by a high degree of personal intimacy, emotional depth, moral commitment, social cohesion and continuity in time. Community is founded on man conceived in his wholeness rather than in one or another of the roles, taken separately, that he may hold in a social order. It draws its psychological strength from levels of motivation deeper than those of mere volition or interest, and it achieves its fulfilment in a submergence of individual will that is not possible in unions of mere convenience of rational assent. Community is a fusion of feeling and thought, of tradition and commitment, of membership and volition. It may be found in, or be given symbolic expression by, locality, religion, nation, race, occupation or crusade. Its archetype, both historically and symbolically, is the family, and in almost every type of genuine community the nomenclature of family is prominent. Fundamental to the strength of the bond of community is the real or imagined antithesis formed in the same social setting by the non-communal relations of competition or conflict,

utility or contractual assent. These, by their relative impersonality and anonymity, highlight the close personal ties of community.[10]

A number of comments must be made on this sociological concept of community:

1. It does not exist exclusively in small groups but, in most instances, it can only exist in a large group when that group is composed of small groups in which intimacy already exists.

2. Symbolic ritual is almost an inevitable result of the intimacy described and, in its turn, it reinforces the intimacy. Sociologists would say to the theologian that if there are some kind of tenuous links of intimacy between people, liturgy will reinforce those links and then the liturgy itself will become more meaningful. The link between community and liturgy, therefore, is one of reciprocal causality, though liturgy can only have its impact if there are at least traces of community to begin with.

3. Community can never be effectively sought as an end in itself. Much of the "search for community" in the modern world is doomed to failure precisely because intimacy is not an end but rather a result. A group of human beings come together to accomplish some common purpose. If the purpose is nothing more than community itself then the group of human beings is without substantive purpose and will quickly fall apart. Even in the most intimate communities, that between husband and wife, the intimacy they hope for results from common efforts rather than from direct search.

4. The intimacy of community is not easy either to achieve or to sustain. As I have pointed out elsewhere, privacy and spontaneity are frequently difficult to maintain in the face of strong community pressures. Furthermore, the experience of intimacy frequently recalls the unresolved conflicts of our familial past, particularly when a community does not have a clearly defined set of goals and purposes. Many small collegial communities in the contemporary Church become hotbeds of neuroses precisely because the members of the community turn the group into replications of their own families with all the problems and

[10] Robert Nisbet, *The Sociological Tradition* (New York, 1966), pp. 47–48.

conflicts of the family backgrounds. Attempts at intimacy, then, are risky, save for the mature.

From these points one can conclude that liturgy strengthens and reinforces community and ought to help the tenuous bonds of intimacy become strong and permanent. It ought, further, to keep the minds and the wills of the members of the community on the directed course of their common goal. Furthermore, it ought to provide them with some of the emotional strength that they need to resist regression to infantile behaviour patterns. One must note that the Christian liturgy, designed as it is to symbolize the love which Christians believe is the core of the universe, ought to be particularly well equipped to achieve these goals. If it has not done so, one of the reasons may be that theologians have talked glibly about the relationships among symbolism, liturgy and community but have not understood the complexity of these relationships.

It is frequently objected that small communities are dangerous because they tend to turn in on themselves and ignore the world beyond their own narrow limits. That there is an inclination to gnosticism in small groups is undeniable, but one would presume that the Lord sent the Holy Spirit to the Church which, incidentally, *was* a small group, so that the Spirit could prevent the Christian community from becoming narrow and inward looking. There is no reason in the nature of things why small groups must look merely inward. It is, on the contrary, the role of the Spirit and the role of the leadership of the Church to challenge Christian communities to a vision of the world beyond their own limited boundaries. A small-group Christian community merely provides the symbolic base on which its members can stand and from which they can venture forth to the world beyond. The large, impersonal Sunday congregation neither provides such a base nor moves very many of its members to the world beyond.

The world view and the ethos enacted in the Eucharist are designed, rather, to persuade its initiates that the Love which is at the core of the Real is so intense and so powerful that it cannot be pent up within one small group but must flow out from that small group "even to the end of the earth".

John Tinsley

Liturgy and Art

I. Incarnation Art and Liturgy

CHRISTIAN theologians, including liturgiologists, have on the whole shown an inclination to cultivate closer relations with philosophers, especially metaphysicians, rather than artists, poets, dramatists. In particular, there has been a Christian preference for what William F. Lynch has called "the men of the infinite"[1] rather than "the men of the finite". By the men of the infinite Lynch means the idealists, the romanticists, the men of the large generalization or abstraction. On the other hand, there are "the men of the finite", the positivists, the men of fact, detail, empirical reality. It is odd that a religion centred on the Incarnation, the Word become flesh, should, even in its apologetic statements, have shown this propensity towards philosophy. One might have expected it to have had a special sensitivity to the arts in general and to the verbal arts in particular, and to have been unusually solicitous about language and its use, with a deep sense of its potency and influence. The closest association might have been expected between the theologian and those whose life is to work with words, the poets. It has taken the Christian religion a long time to place art at the centre of its cognitive activity, and not on the periphery as something which is marginal to human life, basically decorative and recreational. It is this attitude which has led to the "use" of art for evangelistic or didactic purposes, rather than treating it as a source of truth, including theological truth, in its own right. This preoccupation with evangelism and

[1] William F. Lynch, *Christ and Apollo* (New York, 1960).

pedagogy is one of the reasons why Christianity has found it so difficult to be related to the arts in terms of genuine freedom and equality. Clerical possessiveness has frequently attempted to use the arts in a complacent and self-righteous manner ("always for the Lord's sake"). There is a parallel in the Church's relations with education where again proprietary guardianship has inhibited attachment to education for its own sake. As regards the liturgy, this has often inhibited the Church from setting the liturgy free to be itself. Concepts of authority and "validity" have been interpreted in a static backward-looking and "archaeological" way—allowing the past to be so oppressively normative for the present as to prevent spontaneity and dim eschatological perspective.

There is a mimetic element in the liturgy but this needs always to be interpreted in dynamic terms. Just as the *imitatio Christi* motif has suffered from literalism and antiquarianism, so too with the element of imitation in the liturgy. The imitation of Christ, as the life of Christ which, through the Spirit, is lived out in and through the lives of believers, is a dynamic growing process, a continuous enlargement of experience. The history of art provides useful reminders of the positive creative features of imitation in the hands of the artist. An artist can imitate the subject and style of another artist in a way which produces something new; it is not necessarily a literal slavish copying. Similarly, the liturgy is not an attempt to reproduce the static past of a still life but is, so to speak, a temporary halt on a continuing journey. To ignore the organic relation between liturgy and art is to surrender an important insight already present in the Fathers. There is a significant patristic exploration for instance in Augustine, of the Incarnation as *the* art form of God, the paradigm of human creativity. Moreover, there are full resources in the Christian doctrinal tradition for a development of a doctrine of man as pro-creator, in freedom and inventiveness, of a kind which would have paid rich dividend in the contemporary discussion of "man come of age", "human maturity" and "secularization".

To speak of the Incarnation as an art form is no mere rhetoric. The subject of the Incarnation is undoubtedly one who works with words as a poet and in human actions as a dramatist. He is correctly to be described as a *dramatic* poet who necessarily and not accidentally communicates through parabolic words and deeds. The Incarnation has the austerity, the self-giving in love, of the artist, and also the quality of waiting upon God. It is not self-declaratory or self-identifying in a propagandist fashion. The Incarnation is "mystery" in the sense that what might seem to be foolish and ineffective is, to the perception of faith, wisdom and power.

The Christian liturgy is rooted in the action of this Incarnation. It is imitative of it in a quite distinctive Christian sense. Not, that is to say, that the liturgy is some archaic exercise whereby, in a literal fashion, the Incarnation is re-enacted *de novo*. But imitative in a creative sense, for which the best term is Luther's *conformitas* (which is itself a return to a Pauline emphasis). It is not so much a matter of Christians in the liturgy going through certain actions which in the manner of "sympathetic magic" bring about the thing being mimed. But rather that the one God does in the Eucharist what he did in Christ: moulds (through the Spirit) human life along the lines of the humanity he achieved in Christ. The liturgy is seen by the Christian as the paradigm of all art forms and of man's creativity in imitative but nevertheless creative dependence on the Incarnation. The liturgy is a composite art-form containing man's significant speech, gesture, song and dance before God. It thus appears as the basic rehearsal of human life as genuinely personal life in community, its essential quality being the *koinonia*: the deep personal reciprocal character of the common life in the body of Christ. This is the fundamental pattern for the "hominization" of human life: a community of freedom and trust. This is the pattern *mimesis* of the meaning and destiny of man as the Christian sees it which is, as W. B. Yeats put it, that man cannot know the truth as his personal private possession but can only embody it, or, in the words of Antoine de St Exupéry, truth is not what we discover but what we create.

The Incarnation draws together in Christian thinking the creation of God and the creativity of man in such a way as to produce the distinctive character of the Christian doctrine of the pro-creatorship of man. The signs of this pro-creatorship the Christian believer descries in man's scientific and artistic endeavour. All art therefore in his eyes has liturgical potential. The necessity of art for human fruition is an aspect of the necessity of liturgy.

II. Cult and Culture

If it may be accepted that the structure of the liturgy is essentially that of an art-form, what does this imply about the manner and content of its celebration?

First of all, form and content need to be so integrated that neither can be conceived without the other. The Eucharist is a symbolic action and not a concept, although some phases of eucharistic theology, would give one the impression that it is entirely the latter. The Eucharist is fundamentally a symbol which arose out of another symbol. The Eucharist is a cluster of symbolic words and actions through which the presence of that which is symbolized is experienced as a living reality.

The liturgy as an art-form means that there is something in it for everybody. The liturgy cannot be regarded as only and ever a domestic matter for "insiders" only. The liturgy for insiders only might be defensible in a primary missionary situation where initiation involves a rather drastic transfer from one cultural inheritance to another. But in contemporary society we are in a "secondary" missionary situation in the sense that western Europe has been christianized. The "priestly" task of the Church in such a situation is to allow the liturgy to be the means of so presenting a perspective on human life and experience that disclosures of Christian meaning are made possible. This will mean an austerity of form and manner, and an economy of style which allows the participant to "read between the lines" in varying degrees, and not a private esoteric language and style which can only be deciphered by an educated minority of "insiders".

This probably means that there could now be a specially close link between cult and culture not as the means of fostering some new art-form, in the way one traces the development of drama from the rite of the Mass, but to nourish and sustain the astringency and asceticism that an increasingly barbarous culture necessitates for its reformation. By a barbarous culture, I mean one which by its casualness and obviousness impoverishes life by seeking responses only of an undemanding uncreative kind, trivializes serious issues into banality and blurs the distinction between reality and fantasy. Could the cult become the foyer of a new culture drawing its strength from the reality and realism of the Incarnation and so renewing and redeeming society from settling for a flat and neutral image of man that seldom in its sensitivity touches the heights and depths of reality as the Christian knows them?[2]

III. Liturgy and Language

To turn to the specific question of liturgy and language, Christians are defined in the epistle of James as "poets of the Word" (1.22: *poētai logou*) and liturgy can be seen as a foyer wherein one learns that if it is true that to bury oneself in a lexicon is to arise in the presence of God,[3] it is all the more true that to learn the rich polysemous character of words is one of the chief ways of doing homage to the Word who became flesh and worked with words as poet.

Liturgy belongs to literature because it uses words in a literary, that is metaphorical, way, and arranges them in a significant pattern, so that they assume a particular tone of voice. I am reminded of the intimate relationship between the two by Richard Hoggart, who in his essay "Why I value literature"[4] speaks of it as being more than the exploration of human experience and characterizes it, significantly for us, as a "contemplating" or "celebrating" of human experience. It is interesting to note how often the creative artist, whether writer or painter, when speaking of the creative process as he experiences it, makes use of terms from the vocabulary of religion.

The essence of the literary use of language is metaphor, using words so that one meaning of a word is "carried across" (μεταφόρα) to another. It is here that we would locate the process of "hominization" in both religion and literature. There are those who believe that the cosmos is now so "desacralized" and "disenchanted" that the use of metaphor in human language is

[2] See William F. Lynch, *The Image Industries* (London, 1960).
[3] E. C. Hoskyns, *Cambridge Sermons* (London, 1938).
[4] Richard Hoggart, *Speaking to each other*, vol. II (London, 1970).

hopelessly *démodé*. The use of metaphor, says Alain Robbe-Grillet, takes one half-way to religion by implying a fundamental unity of things which makes possible the exchange by which metaphor exists. But this, argues Robbe-Grillet, implies a relationship between man and his environment which does not exist.

This side of the grave, worship inevitably means metaphor. To make a straight equation of the kind all life = worship (and therefore no particular act in a particular place, no holy times and no holy places) is anticipatory eschatology with a vengeance! To say that the whole of our life is automatically worship is to try to jump out of our finite skins. Moreover, in Christian liturgy which necessitates a narrative element because of the story on which it is based, there is bound to be an allegorical quality. By this I mean that the story of the liturgy will have one surface meaning for the outsider who drops in (a collection of people going through the words and motions of some cult) but another underlying life for the believing participants, a "secondary world" of meaning. So that the liturgy is allegorical in the literal sense of speaking in public (ἄλλος ἀγορεύω) about something else.

What should be the "tone of voice" in our contemporary liturgical use of language? Perhaps we can find a clue by reflecting on the change in tone in poetry between, e.g., T. S. Eliot and his immediate predecessors. After the "sweet", "poetic", "mellifluous", exalted style of a predecessor like Binyon or Masefield, the language and tone of T. S. Eliot's "Waste Land" came as a shock with its "concrete", "dissonant", abrasive style. If the contemporary Church is not able to respond to the resplendent majestic monumentalism of, say, late Gothic or Baroque architecture, neither is it able to respond readily, to use an English example, to the splendid majestic incantatory quality of Cranmer's Anglican liturgy. The quest for "beautiful" language in religion (like the desire for "beautiful" church buildings) can often conceal a docetic dislike for the concrete realities of human bodily existence, and such an attitude is diametrically opposed to all that the Incarnation stands for.

This concern with the tone of voice of liturgical speech is not anti-poetic; it is restiveness with *a particular kind* of poetry.

Eliot's own style is very much the poetic use of language! The present Christian discontent with much inherited liturgical language is that it is too exaltedly majestic, too self-consciously "numinous", particularly for an incarnational religion. If, as the American poet Wallace Stevens says, the natural momentum of the human mind is all towards abstraction, this is precisely where the Christian sees redemption as being most needed. This is the world of the "men of the infinite" and the human mind needs to be turned back again and again to the particular, the concrete, the real. The sacred is to be perceived not in some "spiritual" world which exists above or alongside present existence without ever coming into real contact with it, but precisely in the bodily, the material, the created. The Incarnation is God's care for the particular and concrete and the response to it is most appropriately a liturgy which celebrates a real engagement with the world. Poetry is natural to liturgy not because of some self-conscious desire to sound religious, awestruck, but the natural consequence of a deeply felt belief that precisely in things as they are "secondary worlds" of meaning are to be descried.

I referred above to the story element in the movement of the traditional Christian liturgy and suggested that this narrative framework gave it an allegorical character. The allegorical interpretation has been taken to extravagant and improbable lengths in the past, like, it is significant to note, the allegorical interpretation of parables. But just as excesses in the latter ought not to be taken to mean that there is no element of allegory in any of the parables of Jesus, so it would be a violation of its form (as a pattern of metaphorical speech and symbolic gesture) to suggest that there is nothing allegorical in liturgy. Here again is a crucial question in the area of cult and culture. If there are forces hostile to metaphor, the same is true of story. There are those who say, for instance, that the novel is now dead because it is based on the assumption that to tell a story presupposes a meaningful pattern to life. A story with a beginning and an ending implies a framework of progression, inter-related events and meaning. But this is to make a presupposition about human life which is no longer tenable. Whether it be drama or the novel, something amorphous, without plot or progression (like *Waiting for Godot*) is more to the point of cosmic pointlessness. The story-form implies an unwarrantable intrusion of meaning and the unpremeditated happening is more germane to modern nihilism.

This is the crux of the question of the *humanum* in man. To bring about a state of affairs where the telling of the story or the impulse to metaphor is no longer required because no longer relevant is to dehumanize man in a radical way, since he is fundamentally a metaphor-making animal and story-teller. Further, far from being inimical to spontaneity, story-telling is its very basis. Genuine spontaneity is not possible in some sort of isolated "contemporariness" which is not in continuous dialogue with both the past and the future. The conditions for genuine spontaneity and genuine contemporaneity are the same and have never been better expounded than by T. S. Eliot,[5] what he says about poetry being true also of liturgy:

> The historical sense involves a perception, not only of the pastness of the past, but of its presence. . . . This historical sense, which is a sense of the timeless as well as of the temporal together, is what makes a writer traditional. And it is at the same time what makes a writer most acutely conscious of his place in time, of his contemporaneity.

The liturgy needs to be both traditional and contemporary, both a story and a happening, existentialist, yes, in the sense of an entire personal commitment in the present but not in the sense of having no perspective on the past.

[5] T. S. Eliot, "Tradition and the individual talent", *The Sacred Word* (London, 1960), p. 49.

Günter Rombold

Creative Freedom in the Parish Church

DOES a church really have to be the most boring place you can think of? A place you go to out of a sense of duty and convention in order to listen to sermons in the dead old language of who knows how long ago, and sing hymns that not even grave-dust could dance to? A place where everyone sits to be counted in his pew and only the priest, minister or whatever he's called in any particular case is the only one *doing* anything? "What are these churches now but the vaulted sepulchres of God?"[1] There's no doubt that divine service as celebrated all over the place for a century and a half was an initial symptom of the Deity's death rattle. All it expressed was a Christianity reduced to morality and duty, a church in which only the clergy had the right to be active, and a parish wholly under the influence of the individualism typical of the age. No wonder that creativity expired in such mausoleums. No accident that church architecture came from ages past and that the vulgar and the sentimental conspired to smother art.

Some would say that all that's changed now. We've got a renewed liturgy and a modern style of ecclesiastical design. Thousands of "modern" churches have been built in the last twenty years. We've put up steel and concrete cathedrals—some of which count as spectacular (some might even say masterpieces).

Nevertheless, in the last few years there has been increasingly widespread uneasiness about this kind of building, which so emphatically announces the Church's claim to attention and

[1] Friedrich Nietzsche, *Die fröhliche Wissenschaft.*

newfound validity. Many if not all of these recent churches now seem symbolic of an obsolete image of the Church—of one that shuts itself up in strong keeps and defences instead of taking its chances in the open and looking for dialogue and confrontation. These skyscraping towers, massive blocks of masonry and concrete temples repel rather than invite us in. It all makes you ask whether the Church should not be concerning itself with a more profound kind of creativity instead of saying, as it were, "Look how modern we are now!" Perhaps the Church should start from the parish community whose faith is the source of its creative action.

I. The Church as the Community House

Here we are on biblical ground. We know from the Acts of the Apostles that Christians rejected the temple of the ancient world: "The God who made the world and everything in it... does not live in shrines made by man" (Acts 17. 24). God lives not in buildings but in men: "Do you not know that *you* are God's temple and that God's Spirit dwells in you? If any one destroys God's temple, God will destroy him. For God's temple is holy, and that temple you are" (1 Cor. 3. 16, 17).

Therefore the first buildings which Christians put up were not God's houses but community houses. By chance, part at least of one of these early Christian centres has survived—at Dura-Europos. It is a house containing several rooms; the exact purpose of only one of them, the baptismal chamber, has been determined. Christian houses of this kind were certainly more closely related to Jewish community houses and synagogues than to Greek and Roman temples.

In the reign of Constantine the situation changed. The *ecclesia pressa* became the well-known Imperial Church and the small parishes grew into a mass-Church. But here the connection was not, structurally, with the temples of times past; the basilicas were massive assembly halls. Augustine defined church architecture thus: "*Ecclesia dicitur locus quo ecclesia congregatur*".[2]

This, too, is the starting-point for our own attempts to give church-building a theological basis. Hence the Anglican

[2] Augustine, *Quaest. in Heptat.*, 3, 57, p. 289.

theologian Peter Hammond says: "The church building is the house of the Church, in the biblical sense of that word; the house of the people who are themselves the temple of the living God, the habitation of the Spirit; a spiritual house built of living stones."[3] From a radical pastoral viewpoint Bishop Bekkers characterized the church as essentially "a kind of great living-room, a place where the faithful come together to meet the Lord, and one another in the Lord."[4] Frédéric Debuyst has most tellingly developed the conception of the church as the community church; I shall go into his ideas in more detail in this article.

The basic idea of the community house has been stressed in very different ways. Three significant examples will show what I mean.

II. Social Service Centres

In 1968 the Church of England parish of Hodge Hill, Birmingham, built a church in conjunction with a youth centre; the concept is remarkable in many respects.[5] The erection of the building was preceded by some years of discussion between the parish and the Institute for the Study of Worship and Religious Architecture of Birmingham University from which the first thing to emerge was the pastoral concept. The actual design came from the Birmingham School of Architecture.

The complex has become a Church service centre for the entire sector of the city. The main hall is used for services on Sunday, but on weekdays it is open to the parish for many different purposes. There is also a sports hall and a number of smaller rooms. The centre is really in use all day. It has become a first-class point of attraction for the young people of the neighbourhood. Of course, this is possible only because there are two full-time youth workers and forty voluntary helpers attached to the centre.

The design of the centre is quite unlike the usual church. From outside it looks like a couple of very wide hall-type buildings, with a presbytery nearby. Once inside, you can see the

[3] Peter Hammond, *Liturgy and Architecture* (London, 1960), p. 28.

[4] Bishop Bekkers, quoted by F. Debuyst, *op. cit. infra*, p. 9.

[5] The church at Hodge Hill was described in *The Architects' Journal* (London, 8 Oct. 1969), pp. 875 ff. and in *Christliche Kunstblätter* (Linz, 1969), pp. 85 ff.

immense emphasis put on good lighting and the sort of materials that have a warm and domestic effect (above all bricks and wood). Most of the furnishings are mobile, so that the seats, for example, can be made to face the altar or, turned 90°, the stage. If there's a party the old folk can sit at tables, and the young people have room to play table-tennis. The total effect of the interior is to make one feel at home and to prompt you (as at home) to do different things. Admittedly most parishes today would hesitate at first before doing something "worldly" or "profane" in the room used for divine service. At most a concert seems admissible—as long as it isn't jazz or pop. But that not only young people nowadays but the whole of Christendom until the end of the Middle Ages, and to some extent until the eighteenth century, thought differently was brought out by J. G. Davies in a thorough examination of the question two years ago.[6] Davies formulated the spiritual prerequisites for a conception such as that of the multi-purpose church in Hodge Hill.

It is, of course, impossible for anyone to forget that the expressions of parish life and hence the functions of a parish centre are not the same nowadays as they were in times past. Today no church offers the right of asylum, and no church is now (as in the Middle Ages) used for tithes or markets on saints' days.

The Hodge Hill parish started from the assumption and conviction that its task was pre-eminently social and thus Christian: service to the people of the neighbourhood. This means that the various individuals and groups concerned are faced with a number of possibilities. For the architect the task is more difficult, since his problems increase with the number of required functions. It must be emphasized that a "multi-purpose space" is no all-purpose space, unless one is to construct a wholly functionless hall that is entirely without consciously purposeful form or character. Rooms are required that have a certain architectonic emphasis, but which offer freedom; which arouse the imagination but do not constrain it.

III. Places for Creative Confrontation

The participants in the First International Congress on

[6] J. G. Davies, *The Secular Use of Church Buildings* (London, 1968).

Religion, Architecture and the Visual Arts, held in New York in 1967, will never forget the "happening" that they witnessed in the Judson Memorial Church in Greenwich Village. It was arranged by two of the "fathers" of the modern happening, Lawrence Kornfeld and Al Carmines, who thoroughly transformed the church for the purpose.

What exactly did we experience in the space of a single hour? On entering, you were kissed by a coloured girl, forced up some stairs where you had to eat some unidentifiable kind of soup, and then put on trial under brilliant searchlights. You were chased through a jungle of polystyrene foam and corrugated paper, put up against a wall and photographed with arms outspread, interrogated, led on to the dance-floor by a girl who turned out to be a man, and finally asked by a doctor to put out your tongue, only to be given the verdict of imminent death. These were only a few of the stations on this way of absurdity that we had to follow, poised between rage and laughter.

What was the meaning of all this? Harvey Cox, who was one of the group, wrote a short article in which he warned against any excessive interpretation of the occasion. "It was an experience of uncertainty, anger, eroticism, confusion, fun. It asked nothing else of us...." Yet "we lived through something that nourished us, sharpened our perception, broke open some of our conventional ways of looking at things."[7] It was (an obviously very American) version of something of the absurdity of life scrambled into one of its hours, something akin to Kafka's *The Castle*.

But why did all this take place in a church? My reply would be: Why not? Why shouldn't a church be the place in which we are confronted with everything that is beautiful and repressive, intelligible and inconceivable in our lives? Or is a church an island to retreat to from life's problems? Didn't the Middle Ages celebrate its holy and unholy games—for instance, the Feast of Fools—in the churches?

Of course all this could take another direction: that of discussion, of confrontation of the Christian conscience with the political reality of our own times. The Swiss architect Walter M.

[7] Harvey Cox, "Kinesthetic Happening: Art or Atrocity", in *Revolution, Place and Symbol* (New York, 1969), pp. 216 ff.

Förderer makes a plea for this course when he says: "If churches still have to be built at all, then they must be places of confrontation, i.e., more than places for directed meditation and receptive prayer. They should not be the locations of a merely abstract form of celebration or even mystification, but locations of reality amid other realities.... In regard to the fruitful tension existing within the Church, and in consideration of the democratic society, there must be entirely new experiments in church-building: experiments outside the established ecclesiastical centres; architectural improvisations in places which, as municipal centres, have for a long time been more important than the so-called centres of ecclesial institutions."[8] Förderer speaks of the "church" in the urban garage, in the railway station, in densely-populated residential quarters or at big exhibitions.

Evidently, the "church as the location of creative confrontation" can mean many different things: formalistic or political confrontation. Political confrontation holds the promise of chances and problems: the chance to overcome the "threshold shyness" that prevents many people from even entering a church, but also the danger of abuse or of manipulation. Very careful consideration must also be given to the question of where people nowadays like to get together and where they don't (a block of flats, for instance, is usually out of the question), if another situation of exclusivity is not to result.

The formalistic confrontation can often go further. The happening in New York raised questions of deeper moment than our conventional politicians are usually able to make us ask. Of course this happening is only mentioned as an example of all the possible forms and actions in which the barriers between "art" and life can be cancelled. This is basically the tendency of all modern art, so that entirely new possibilities of confrontation with life are available. In this way it should be possible to connect the various individual dimensions of our lives.

IV. Places to celebrate the Paschal Mystery

I shall never forget Holy Saturday night with the students of

[8] Walter M. Förderer, "Zentren politischer Urbanität", in Hans-Eckehard Bahr, *Kirchen in nachsakraler Zeit* (Hamburg, 1968), pp. 114 ff.

Nijmegen. During the three hours every conceivable medium was brought into use. Slides were projected on three large screens, playlets were acted, songs in three languages—English, French and Dutch—were sung. Classical music and negro spirituals were alternated and went very well together. The big questions of human life came alive: Where do we come from—creation; where are we going?—death and resurrection. Everyone sat unmoving and quiet as images of daybreak were shown, and finally the students broke out into a joyful Alleluia! and everyone said Shalom! to his neighbour.

If the church is the community house then this house must provide space for the community feasts and celebrations before all else. In a feast the community celebrates the significance of its existence; it experiences life as a costly gift and says Yes and Amen to it.[9] At every feast there is something worth celebrating, something that is celebrated. If we celebrate a friend's birthday, we are trying to show him in this way what he means to us, that he is close to us. We give expression to the joy we feel that our friend is alive at all, that he's still alive, that he's still among us. This kind of feast makes something shine out on to our everyday life which helps us to overcome its depressing uniformity, boredom and turgidity. Plato said that feasts were a gift of the gods to enable men to get straight about things again, and become reorientated.[10]

The Christian community celebrates the mystery of the Passover. We rejoice that the Lord is alive and dwells in our midst. This is a revelation of our lives' significance: the divine Yes has been spoken to man.

I have already intimated that little of this spirit is discernible in most of the eucharistic feasts in our parishes. The pentecostal fire of the Christian feast is very much damped down, and even the liturgical renewal hardly ever succeeds in fanning the embers. Why is this? Because we have given far too little thought to how modern man celebrates a feast, how he sings songs, what instruments he plays, what kind of pictures and what sort of rooms he likes. The absurd and ultimately inhuman rejection of the body by nineteenth-century Christians also drove art from our churches.

[9] Josef Pieper, *Zustimmung zur Welt* (Munich, 1963).
[10] Plato, *Nomoi*, 635 c–d.

If we are afraid to let contemporary art into our churches, to allow the rhythms of our music to be heard in them, if we won't give free play to imagination once again, then the whole liturgical renewal will be unable to reach the men of the present. We just have to say Yes to the wager that's involved in all this, as Harvey Cox has told us in his marvellous book on festivity and fantasy.[11]

If the celebration of the paschal mystery is "the summit towards which the activity of the Church is directed, and at the same time the fountain from which all her power flows",[12] then the rooms in which the parish community assembles must allow something of the spirit of this celebration to be felt. This is why Frédéric Debuyst insists that the community house should be a "paschal meeting-room", a room of encounter which obtains its significance and atmosphere from the paschal mystery.[13]

Debuyst believes that the really good churches of the future should look more like ordinary houses and not like the churches of the past and the present. He combines his theological postulates with a remarkable phenomenology of the modern house, which is no longer there, like the house of earlier epochs, to offer protection, but to provide space for human communication. The modern living-room is multi-applicable, and therefore tends to versatility and mobility, thus favouring human creativity.

Of course, the comparison between the community house and the modern house ought not to be taken too far: what is important in this regard is the idea of the house as a centre of communication and not the imitation of external forms. It is also a question of showing that the activity of the community reaches its summit in the celebration, and that therefore the rooms should also have a festive character. (Naturally this doesn't mean fancy decoration and overplaying the atmosphere in any way. The framework of Christian festivity should be simple. My own opinion is that the wholly spiritual simplicity of the Cistercians has given us some of the most beautiful churches,

[11] Harvey Cox, *The Feast of Fools. A Theological Essay on Festivity and Fantasy* (Cambridge, Mass., 1969).

[12] Vatican II, *Constitutio de sacra liturgia*, 10.

[13] Frédéric Debuyst, *Modern Architecture and Christian Celebration* (London, 1968), p. 19 *et passim*.

refectories and cloisters of the Middle Ages.) If these ideas are accepted then our parishes must realize that architecture must undergo a fundamental transformation.

Three model conceptions of church building for the present-day parish have been put forward here. Despite all the differences between them their fundamental similarity should be plain. The church as the community house (although the form of expression may change in specific cases) is always a centre of living communication. It is clear that architectural and artistic emphasis can contribute to making human encounter creative in itself. But this will happen only if no rigid schemes are followed which freeze men and their imagination, and only if the locations made available are conducive to creative freedom.

Translated by John Griffiths

Helmut Hucke

Towards a New Kind of Church Music

MANY Christians are saying nowadays that Church music is threatened with extinction. Some organizations specializing in Church music have even become platforms for the more outspoken critics of liturgical renewal. What are these critics saying? The renewal of the liturgy, they claim, has given rise to an unparalleled betrayal of our cultural heritage in the sphere of music. The musical tradition of the Church has been imperilled by a superficial understanding of the meaning of "active participation" in the liturgy and by the use of the language of the people. The true art of Church music is being replaced by experimentation by amateurs and the invasion of, for example, "jazz" in the church is inevitably leading to a rapid banishment of the sacral sphere as a whole. A typical recent criticism is that "the musical structure of the *Missa Romana*, which has hitherto been so artistic . . . is being devalued both theologically and musically" and that this devaluation has "its roots in the anthropocentric character of our contemporary liturgy".[1] The same author says later in his article: "individual church musicians and cathedral and church choirs—these are the only bastions still left standing, unless they too have, in the meantime, already fallen victims to an unenlightened process of liturgical renovation".[2]

Church Music as a Tradition

The view that the Church has a traditional repertory of music

[1] J. Overath, "Sinn und Würde der Musica sacra", in *Musica sacra—CVO*, 88 (1968), p. 246. [2] *Ibid.*, p. 248.

to preserve or that there is any such traditional repertory at all and any need to foster it is quite recent. It goes back to the rediscovery of the Church music of the "early Italian school", represented especially by the work of Palestrina, the so-called Raphael of music, which was regarded as the ideal of pure, authentic Church music. This rediscovery was in fact first made by men of letters and amateur musicians at the beginning of the romantic movement. The music of Palestrina and his contemporaries was only gradually taken up by professional musicians and almost a century elapsed before it became widely used in the Church.

Those who supported this historical form of Church music felt at first far less committed to the repertory as such and more drawn to use it rather as an example of musical style, which had to be developed further. One of the first men to weld this attempt to restore the early music of the Church in this way into an organized movement, the "Universal Society of St Cecilia" (*Allgemeiner-Cäcilien-Verein*), and to draw the attention of Rome to the movement was Franz Xaver Witt. He saw his task as: "first to make the world aware of the great merits of the early musicians by the spoken and written word and by action and then to draw attention to its shortcomings, in order to let art progress".[3] He also appealed, round about this time, for a "modern Palestrina"—clearly regarding himself as that composer.[4]

It was not until research into the history of music had reached a fairly advanced stage of development and more and more early music had been re-edited and published that increasing emphasis came gradually to be placed on fostering early Church music as such, as distinct from regarding it purely as a stylistic ideal. In other words, the original idea of musical composition based on a traditional model led to the later idea of possessing, preserving and fostering the whole repertory of that tradition.

Gregorian chant is another case in point. It is quite wrong to think that this was the "real music" of the Church for centuries.

[3] *Musica sacra*, 13 (1880), p. 3.

[4] "I am bold enough to claim that not a single one of my compositions is at variance with the fundamental mood and pattern of Gregorian chant . . . On the contrary, by no means all my pieces would fit into a Mass by Palestrina as *intermezzi* . . . The better works in the 'style of Witt' are much, much closer to Gregorian chant than many of the works in the style of Palestrina. *Qui capere potest, capiat* . . ." *Musica sacra*, 10 (1877), p. 132.

It is, for example, not mentioned at all in the Tridentine documents on Church music. The Fathers of the Council discussed the question of *musica* in the Church in the twenty-second session and passed a resolution in which it was simply stated that nothing lascivious or impure should take place in *cantu* or in *organo*.[5] For the Council of Trent, then, the problems of *musica* were the problems of the music of the Church during the sixteenth century. The Fathers were certainly not concerned with the problems of Gregorian chant or its use in church in their debate on music. In the resolutions passed during the twenty-third session, when the training of priests was debated, we read, in connection with Gregorian chant, that candidates being trained for the priesthood should learn grammar, *cantus* and *computus ecclesiasticus* as well as other useful arts.[6] It is clear, then, that Gregorian chant was not regarded as a kind of Church music and above all not as the stylistic norm for music in the Church. It was not *musica* at all, but *cantus*, in other words, one of the ritual duties of the clergy.

It was not until the pontificate of Pius IX in the nineteenth century that an "authentic edition" of Gregorian chant was published for the first time in connection with the attempts being made at that period to exercise a central control over the liturgy. The authenticity of this edition was less applicable to the chant itself than to the question of the liturgical ordering of the melodies. What is more, this edition was based, not on the ancient manuscripts, but on the *Editio Medicaea*. This document was commissioned as a result of the Council of Trent, but was eventually published privately.

It was the Solesmes revival and this movement's debate about the "authentic edition" which led to the development of a sense of tradition in Gregorian chant and, in the question of the "authentic edition", to the eventual publication of the *Editio Vaticana* of 1905 ff.[7] Both this long debate about authenticity and the problem of copyright in turn led to the conviction that a liturgical melody or a definite version of a melody could be laid

[5] *Concilium Tridentinum*, ed. *Societas Goerresiana, Actorum* pars V, Sessio XXII, 963.

[6] *Ibid*., pars VI, 597.

[7] See P. Combe, *Histoire de la Restauration du Chant grégorien d'après des documents inédits* (Solesmes, 1969).

down juridically and authoritatively in the rubrics. It was therefore only when it had been rediscovered as "early music" and had been assimilated by the professional music "industry" that Gregorian chant came to be treated as an object of musical tradition. Pius XI contrasted it in his Apostolic Constitution *Divini cultus sanctitatem* of 1929 with *Musica sacra*, but it was not until the publication of the Sacred Congregation of Rites' Instruction on Church Music of 1958 that it was defined as a category of Church music.[8]

Church Music as a Sacral Style

For centuries, a distinction has been made between religious and non-religious music in many different societies, both Christian and non-Christian. Very frequently, religious music has been clearly marked off from profane music. Demarcation of this type has usually had the purpose or the result either of designating a certain kind of music, because of its situation in society, as pagan, profane or offensive or of rejecting all beauty and skill in music as sensuous pleasure that was harmful to the soul and its salvation. Even when a distinction was made between a "church style" of music and a "theatrical style" and the style of chamber music in the musical theory of the seventeenth century, no ideal styles were postulated. All that was done was to put social labels on musical styles that had in any case already become familiar.

The idea of a positive sacral style in music originated at the same time as the rediscovery of early Italian Church music as the ideal religious music. The basis of this idea of a sacral style inspired by the ideal of Italian music was that this *musica sacra* was completely different from all other music in man's environment, with the result that it took him out of this world. Anyone who abandoned himself entirely to the impression it made on him was involuntarily lifted up into a higher and immaterial sphere.

A century later, the Church had made this idea of a special sacral music completely her own and was able to justify this by appealing to the aesthetic doctrines based on human emotions.

[8] See H. Hucke, "L'evoluzione del concetta di 'Musica sacra' ", *Rinnovamento liturgico e Musica sacra* (Bibliotheca Ephemerides Liturgicae, Sectio pastoralis 4) (Rome, 1967), pp. 244 ff.

A hundred years ago, Pius IX said: "Sacred music, resounding in the solemn worship of the Church, is able to seize hold of man powerfully and stimulate his devotion, so long as it is in accordance with the spirit and the form of the holiness of the house of God and with the dignity of the sacred action. In this lofty art, above all those whose compositions are worthy of the holiness of the house of God and of the sublimity of the ceremonies are deserving of the highest praise. Their works must be so highly esteemed precisely because they are so far removed from the insipid and profane music of the theatre and because they release souls from the enticements of earthly things and stimulate them to reflect more deeply about supernatural things..."[9]

According to these ideas, then, Church music was a means of arousing pious emotions. The sacral style of music produced these emotions, whereas other styles of music were believed to evoke unsuitable emotions in religious worship. This entirely precludes any direct relationship between Church music and the event of public worship or the action of the worshipping community. The task of the Church musician is to give to all singing and all forms of music used in public worship a style that approaches the ideal of a sacral style as closely as possible. Nor has Church music any real relationship with theology within the framework of this ideal of a sacral style of music.

Church Music as Art

The claim that Church music should be an art is usually based on Pius X's *Motu proprio* on Church music: "*Musica sacra* must be a true art. Otherwise, it cannot have the effect on those who hear it which the Church hopes that it will produce in including music in her liturgy".[10]

Pius X did not, of course, regard the singing of a prayer or a hymn as Church music. By *musica sacra* in his *Motu proprio*, he meant only the music of church choirs and not the singing of the

[9] Pope Pius IX, *Breve, Multum ad movendos animos*, giving his approval to the Universal Society of St Cecilia, 16 December 1870; see J. Overath, *Der Allgemeine Cäcilien-Verband für die Länder der deutschen Sprache, Gestalt und Aufgabe* (Cologne, 1961), pp. 28 ff.

[10] Pope Pius X, *Motu proprio, Tra le sollecitudini*, I, 2.

priest, ministers or people.[11] What is more, the justification of his demand that the music of the Church should be a true art shows clearly that this concept of art cannot be equated with the concept of art that had been developed since the end of the eighteenth century. According to his *Motu proprio*, Pius X's concept of art goes back to an earlier tradition within which "art" was thought of as a technique, a trade or a craft.

In fact, Church music was cut off from the main stream of artistic development by the simple fact that those who supported the movement to restore the early music of the Church insisted on "classical vocal polyphony" as obligatory and were narrowly determined in their attempts to systematize the distinctive characteristics of their sacral style.[12] In this way, the rejection by Church musicians of "theatrical music" became at the same time a refusal to accept all music of the present and of the past which did not conform to the stylistic ideal of "classical vocal polyphony". What is more, aspects that were "alien to the spirit of the Church" were even discovered in Gregorian chant.[13]

The stylistic ideal of "classical vocal polyphony" continued to prevail in Catholic musical circles even after the whole repertory of the centuries was accepted as the heritage and the task of the Church. The art of Church music came to be regarded as the embodiment of the Church's tradition in music. Art became synonymous with the repertory of the Church musician. The enormous gulf separating non-religious music and Church music since the end of the eighteenth century has, to a very great extent, been caused by the Church's rejection of "art for art's sake" and

[11] H. Hucke, *op. cit.*, p. 246.

[12] For example, by a resolution "on the semi-tone interval in Church music" passed during the seventh general assembly at Biberach in 1877.

[13] "My formation as a musician has followed a dogmatic, aesthetic and historical course. In other words, the distinctive qualities of the style of Church music were first made clear to me by dogmatic theology, that is, I learned through dogma how these musical qualities were connected with God's attributes and with our relationships with him and were necessarily derived from the teaching of the Church concerning the spirit of prayer. After this, I turned to history and looked for those qualities in various compositions . . . I found them (a) in Gregorian chant. In this context, I am bound to observe that I regard everything in Gregorian chant that is written to give individual voices a chance to shine—as in the case of so many tracts, graduals and so on—as alien to the spirit of the Church . . ." F. X. Witt, "Mein Bildungsgang", *Musica sacra* 13 (1880), p. 15.

by her setting up of Church music as a "utility" art. "The eighteenth-century idea of 'art for art's sake' lost all understanding of any music that was involved in life itself and had developed as a popular tradition that was not professionally musical. 'Utility' music came to be valued less than a supposedly freely developing art."[14]

It is only very recently and in connection with the criticism of the "amateur Church music" of liturgical renewal that the argument has been heard that purely "utility" music is unworthy of public worship, on the basis of the fact that only the best is good enough for God and that Church music must therefore be "true art" and confined to professional composers. The work of these professional musicians, however, does scant justice to this claim. It hovers between the extremes of middle class musical expression with an imposing façade and vocal polyphony strongly reminiscent of Palestrina but "improved" by a wider range of tonality and modern sound effects. The professionals aim to compose in accordance with the demands made by liturgical renewal by using the old familiar patterns of composition, but adding, for the required "active participation of the people", a massed choral part to be sung in unison, sometimes producing the painful effect of grand opera. The creative imagination of the composer of Church music has also, of course, been paralysed by the fact that his mind is still firmly embedded in the traditional categories of the ordinary, the proper, motets and so on. It has not yet been realized that there can be no real way of expressing Church music artistically until the composer is freed from the bondage of setting these strictly prescribed, although often revised texts of the historically determined cycle of ordinary and proper to music.

There have, however, been objections to the art of music in the liturgy not only from those concerned with Church music, but also from the liturgical movement itself. These scruples are certainly valid wherever art has been used indiscriminately simply for the sake of a musical performance, as, for example, in cases where the celebration of the Eucharist has become a mere vehicle for the singing of a Mass, a musical entertainment with a liturgical accompaniment. But phenomena of this kind do as little

[14] K. G. Fellerer, "Kirchemusik als Brauchtumsmusik", *Musikalisches Brauchtum, Festschrift für Heinrich Lemacher* (Cologne, 1956), p. 30.

justice to the work of art as to public worship and the problem is not so much one of the aesthetics of Church music as one of Church music which has become a profession "industry".

New "Musica Sacra"

One of the most striking phenomena in contemporary music, however, is that *avant-garde* composers are again and again tending to make use of religious texts and themes. Spiritual music is occupying a more important position in musical life and creativity today than it has done for a long time in the past. Programmes of *musica viva* concerts are full of spiritual music. A new *musica sacra*, which many regard as a theological statement, is emerging from *avant-garde* circles in the world of music. This new *musica sacra*, moreover, has nothing in common with the traditional forms of Church music.

The Protestant theologian and composer Dieter Schnebel has proclaimed it as a "*musica sacra* without taboos"[15]—it should, he believes, avoid pious attitudes and the naïve use of religious language. It might foster the venerable heritage of Church music by carrying opposition to it to the extremes or even including it in composition. The material could be enriched by the introduction of alien effects taken from non-religious circles and of non-acoustic, optical elements. The composer could make use of all kinds of elements that are active within him and apply language, for example, phonemes and phonetic or linguistic processes, to his music. In developing and extending his material in this way, the composer could incorporate many different kinds of sounds and even use theatrical or scenic devices to illustrate his enriched material. This kind of *musica sacra* would put its own content into the music itself. "Whatever happens, this type of music has an explosive effect on traditional worship. We should not, however, be afraid of this movement in Church music, since new liturgical forms have to be found. What is more, instead of merely serving the existing situation, which amounts, after all, to little more than a restoration, this new *musica sacra* can provide music for a form of worship in the church of the future, anticipating its completely different and if possible completely secularized

[15] D. Schnebel, "Musica sacra ohne Tabus", *Melos* 35 (1968), pp. 371–376.

form. Spiritual music of this kind would regain its original eschatological character..."

The problem of "art in the liturgy" will therefore in the future no longer have to be regarded as the problem of the autonomous work of art in public worship. The problem of the concept of the work of art, which has troubled aestheticians in the sphere of music for the last century and a half, seems at last to be resolving itself. Music is taking on an entirely new dimension and is confronting liturgists with quite different questions.

New Forms of Singing in Worship

Another very striking phenomenon in the sphere of music today, as remarkable as that of the new *musica sacra* of the *avant-garde* composers, is the almost world-wide popularity of religious singing among the younger generation.[16] Older musicians and those concerned with Church music have tended to associate various types of music with this new kind of religious singing—entertainment music, dance music, popular music, jazz, profane music with an erotic content and so on. It would at first sight appear as though a new branch of the industry of musical consumer goods has opened. The attempt to define this new spiritual singing, in the light of traditional ideas about Church music, as a form of repertory of sacred music is, however, so far not very successful. Many new concepts have been tried out, all equally confusing, such as jazz in the Church, folk-song masses and "rhythmical music".

In the meantime, it is becoming increasingly clear that these new forms of singing in the Church cannot be regarded simply as a new musical repertory. It is obviously not a purely musical phenomenon at all, but the musical expression of the protest movement of the young. Young people are not expressing their protest in a particular *genre* of music or in a special repertory, but by means of a new relationship with music. Their musical repertory is colourful and varied and may include Gregorian chant, anti-war songs, Bach, negro spirituals and *avant-garde* music.[17]

[16] See, for example, the report on jazz and folk music in the liturgy in *Concilium*, 2/5 (Feb. 1969), pp. 69–85 (American edn., vol. 42).

[17] See J. Eisen's Introduction to his anthology, *The Age of Rock. Sounds*

Popular commercialized religious songs with a strongly sentimental flavour are not in this category and the jazz and creole masses, which now occupy a special section in the record catalogues and interest those who like exotic forms of music, are only on the fringe of this movement, forming, as they do, no more than a rather paradoxical attempt at a new musical style.

Young members of the protest movement regard singing as their most direct means of expression and not as an attempt to foster such awe-inspiring forms of Church music as hymns, anthems and so on. It is precisely for this reason that we are, in some countries, enjoying a real rebirth of spiritual singing which is in fact an important event in the history of the Church. Again, because singing in this case is a direct means of expression, it is not taking place in historical forms such as the antiphons and responsories that have hitherto been unquestioningly accepted as the only valid musical categories in the Church's liturgy. On the contrary, this new singing has broken open the historically fixed frontiers and territories of music in the liturgy and created entirely new liturgical forms—just as Gregorian chant created special liturgical forms in the past.

An opening song at the beginning of the service may, for example, require the reading to follow at once, without any intervening rite or gesture. New and broadly based musical forms for assembling the people for worship are being developed and, in this, records and tape recordings are being employed—they are a legitimate means of reproduction in contemporary music and have become part of the composer's material. Very significant, in my opinion, are the many attempts that are being made at present to set the eucharistic prayers to music. Many Christians regard it as unsuitable and have a feeling of deprivation when the singing ceases as soon as the eucharistic prayer opens and begins again when it ends. The musical adaptations of the Gregorian prefaces and canons are often found unsatisfactory and the official texts frequently prove to be literary structures which are ill adapted to musical composition. As a result, the music is frequently composed and the text is written side by side and the liturgy that

of the American Cultural Revolution (New York, 1969); see also L. G. Dowdey, *Journey to Freedom. A Casebook with Music* (Chicago, 1969).

emerges from this attempt, including the eucharistic prayer, is in verse form.

A remarkable fact is that all this began quite often because the people wanted to sing at Mass at the Our Father, thus showing that the human psychological need to sing at least after the spoken eucharistic prayer demanded to be satisfied. Frequently, too, people have tended to sing what could be described as a well-known repertory, that is, something known to almost everyone present, such as an alleluia refrain from a popular film. This is something that certainly did not occur to the authors of the Constitution on the Liturgy at the Second Vatican Council and it is clearly not always in accordance with the spirit of the rites. But this brings us face to face with the real, concrete problem and function of the people's part in singing during worship and it is obvious that our ideas about and our criteria for the whole question of the people's participation in singing in the liturgy and new Church music generally have still to be worked out.

The existence of Church music as such is not threatened, but we have undoubtedly come to the end of the period of restoration in the sphere of Church music. Until now, Church music has been placed in various categories. It has been regarded as the preservation of a tradition. It has been seen as a sacral style of music. It has been thought of as the embodiment of historical forms such as antiphons and responsories, the ordinary and the proper, motets, hymns, preludes and fugues, the organ and the church choir. All these categories are outdated now and it is clear that they were never the timeless and unquestioned foundations of Church music, but only the ideas put forward by the movement to restore the traditional music of the Church. The various institutions concerned with Church music no longer have the task of propagating certain stylistic clichés and musical repertories as the only suitable Church music. What they have to do now is to help worshipping communities to express themselves musically in their own way. The prerequisite for this is, on the one hand, a living relationship with the traditional music of the Church and, on the other, complete openness to the new music.

Translated by N. D. Smith

Cornelis Dippel

Liturgy in the World of the Sciences, Technology and Commerce

1. *Liturgical misgivings.* Even in the agrarian culture liturgy—the business of listening, believing, thinking and praying—was again and again presented as problematical. One has only to think of the sharp-edged strictures uttered by Israel's prophets, by Jesus and by Paul. Today we live in an industrialized culture dominated by natural science, technology, commerce, economic factors and efficiency. Liturgy is subjected continuously to the pressure exerted by the success and assurance of the exact sciences. Liturgical perplexity has nowhere, perhaps, found such spectacular expression as it did when a nation wanted to pray for the three astronauts in difficulty. In the artificial milieu of *homo faber* can we pray in the wake, as it were, of events, when our decisions about everything—machines, technics, policies—have already been taken in advance? The apparatus answers to the information provided by technology: it does not attend upon the Word of God.

2. *The alleged "coming of age" of modern man.* Since Bonhoeffer, all the theologians have been talking about "man come of age". The marriage between modern science and technology has earned the exact sciences the recognition of society but has also brought them under the sway of the State, of commerce, of economics and of what the public hankers after. The industrialized world is now choc-a-bloc with an unavoidable hierarchy of know-how and is specialized to the extreme. Any relation with the integration of living under the Saving Dispensation scarcely exists. Social economists are saying that the ethos of work is de-

fined nowadays by the struggle to gain admission to a higher range of consumption. Never yet has the "surety of salvation", the assurance of our well-being, been so much entrusted to the vicarious enfranchisement of a few experts. Technocracy and bureaucracy threaten our well-being as responsible, adult persons. We live in a euphoric "and so on, and so on" kind of haze. The place of Christian liturgy is taken by the secular belief in an uninterrupted extrapolation of the "trends" in a "standard world" absorbed in a constantly extending process of self-secularization.[1] One of the many meanings of the word "secularization" is: forgotten of God. Liturgy dies. Communication dies. The only communication that succeeds infallibly is to be found in the sphere of commerce, which appeals to man's latent (and insatiable) desires. The needs which originally provided a stimulus to technology have now come to be a product of it. Every culture has the technology that is in keeping with it. The economy, trade and politics govern science and technology.

3. *A new pseudo-religion*. Whether we know it or not, we now worship a new "god": science. Because of the success and the certainty in operation of its methods the public believes that science has got hold of the fundamental nature and being of matter, the cosmos and life and that within the compass of this what is "authentically" real takes place. The necessary conclusion from that is that the impalpable, ungraspable elements of the Christian faith cannot have the character of reality.[2] The temples of this religion are the laboratories, its priests the research workers and investigators of nature, its rites and ceremonies the buttons and switches and instructions for use of the apparatus.[3] The misunderstanding that centres around this uncomprehended god is almost as great as that surrounding the God of Israel, the Father of Jesus Christ. Modern science itself is aware that it can have no ontological pretensions, that it is just an eliminant of reality *in toto* and does no more than describe recurrent and repeatable

[1] H. Kahn and A. J. Wiener, *The year 2000* (New York, 1967), ch. III.
[2] K. Schumann, *Zur Ueberwindung des Säkularismus, Glaube und Forschung* (1950), Vol. 1, pp. 15–38.
[3] Cf. C. F. von Weizsäcker, *Die Tragweite der Wissenschaft* (Stuttgart, 1964), first lecture.

phenomena in a consistent relation. In giving an account of subatomic phenomena, it fails in the objectivizing process: that is to say, it lays claim to general validity but not to being independent of the human observer. This misconception on the part of the public serves to erase history as well as totality. The creation as history is reduced to the mechanism of evolution and to chance. The unique, the "once only", unrepeatable situation is eliminated. The public lives with and by what is recurrent and repeatable and is unaware of any distinction between "physical reality" and what is known as "nature". Thus people very easily drop into a blend, an amalgam, of naturalism and a blind belief in chance, an unbounded misconception with regard both to modern science and to Christian belief in the Creator and Completion of a dynamic reality.[4]

4. *The system of autonomous reason.* This leaves us—in the end—to the dictates of the model described by Descartes in his *Discours de la méthode* (part 6): man as *"maître et possesseur de la nature"*. Leaving aside the fact that no scientist will talk about the domination of nature—he is on home ground only with that part of nature amenable to methodical treatment, namely, "physical reality"—the philosopher Georg Picht[5] proposes a different and contrasting model: the role of the shepherd in tending the flock committed to his care. Thus exploitation and domination are set over against tending and being put in charge—the "dressing" and "keeping" of Genesis 2. 15. Picht confronts this development with the emancipation-movement begun during the Enlightenment, the attempt to grasp the privileges of adult responsibility and freedom (1784, Kant's *"Was ist Aufklärung?"*). He sees as tragic the growth of the system of autonomous reason, because modern technology, by rationalizing everything, forces the world in which we live exclusively into the horizon of objectivity. Man is reduced to *"ratio"* and stripped of all that constitutes him this one, individual human being. It is the ultimate

[4] Cf. C. J. Dippel and J. M. de Jong, *Geloof en Natuurwetenschap*, pt. I; C. J. Dippel, in pt. II: "de ontmoeting van christelijk en exact-natuurwetenschappelijk ethos in een profaniserende cultuur" (the encounter of the Christian ethos with that of the exact sciences in a profanizing culture) (The Hague, 1966/67).

[5] Georg Picht, *Technik und Ueberlieferung* (Furche-Verlag, Hamburg, 1959).

triumph of statistics and the demands of the categorizer. The result is a tremendous reversal for human freedom: the system produces a type of man for whom the possibility no longer exists of controlling, in freedom, the system of autonomous freedom; for man too is absorbed into the system. A technological civilization which is autonomous even *vis-à-vis* man—besides its autonomy *vis-à-vis* God and nature—has become a *real* automatic system. Man's freedom to make decisions is eliminated, history is eliminated and turns into permanent "reproduction", the "and so on" culture which I mentioned earlier on. Something essential has been forgotten. "The forgotten factor is the great imprisonment of man's freedom in his history" (Picht). Living comes to be a totally programmed kind of living. A really automatized system can only terminate in a catastrophe. To judge from experience, we are living permanently on the edge of the abyss. Obviously, we are here a long way off from any association with Christian liturgy.

5. *The flight from responsibility.* We are faced with a choice. Either we live on our own property, in our artificial world, in "private enterprise" or under the dictatorship of the few, without responsibility—or we live each with his fellows the world over in dependence on the Lord of our Salvation, we share our life together, and care for one another's future. We all go on about renewal; but for most of us the price of understanding that the extraordinary potentialities of science and technology are forcing us thoroughly to overhaul the old skill we had for living together is just too high. Everyone has something that has to be preserved at someone else's expense. At the end of the day we look after ourselves and make others the victims.

We see it in the churches: despite the most splendid liturgies the congregation as a fraternity is dying and becoming a fixed collective of individualists, inert, inexpressive, ready to forget God in the community or to identify him with the social order as it is or as they would have it. For believers the Church is the severest trial of all. One notices it also in the "intellectual" difficulties that people have with prayer: reason and logic are employed to demonstrate that science precludes the exercise of faith. It is no matter, therefore, that the theoretical physicist Pascual

Jordan, one of the people responsible for creating the mathematical apparatus of modern physics, can write: "Fundamentally, there lies only an unexpectedly slender and faulty covering or sheet of dependable coerciveness over what occurs in nature—we are treading, as it were, on a thin layer of ice with mysterious and bottomless depths beneath our feet". He has formulated too the "principle of double negation": modern physics says "no" to the classical concepts that at one time were advanced, on a deterministic and materialistic basis, as proof *contra Deum*. This principle supplies no definite answer: we may choose between God and nihilistic chance. For himself, he concludes his book with a reference to Psalm 121.[6] In my experience, these sorts of difficulties over prayer are not going to be met in that way; for one knows that belief in a God to whom one can pray entails what Jesus was talking about in John 21. 18: "another will gird you and carry you where you do not wish to go". We do not want that kind of surrender. We hanker deliberately after a sort of security, which of necessity is more deterministic or entails a programmed existence or nihilism—provided that things go on in the same old way. And so we land up with the "self-running processes" which in science are always regarded as promoting chaos.

We notice it in science as well: "the rationality of science is enhancing the irrational power of those who issue the orders . . . the process of rationalizing the world has served only to intensify the irrationality of the power game to the nth degree".[7] The men of science think they are the productive ones, but they are products: that is, the most characteristic instance of alienation. Every science skirts around the problems which itself creates. In the economic sphere, for example, inflation, that is, the uncontrolled redistribution of assets, scientifically licensed corruption—or the legitimation of the increasing gap between rich and poor, getting rich on the backs of the poor. In technology: the usurious deployment of the complete reduction of a culture to technology, so that technology—in essence an intermediary process—becomes an end in itself. The replacement of man qua auxiliary by a

[6] Pascual Jordan, *Der Naturwissenschaftler vor der religiösen Frage* (Hamburg, 1964), pp. 151–7.

[7] Georg Picht, *Mut zur Utopie* (Piper-Verlag, 1969), p. 93.

machine is acclaimed as an ideal: help yourself, in a flood of energy! "Expansion" is our hope, it is our plain duty to turn everything into a vogue, subjecting everything to the principle of rapid obsolescence, so that production and consumption can go on and on and on: everything, as opposed to the immanent technological ethos, which is aimed at combating waste and superfluity. Meanwhile, democracy is dying—and moral reflection too—in the pace and haste of society; for they cost too much time.

Max Born, one of the pioneers of modern physics, who has always sought to evoke a sense of responsibility, reaches the harrowing conclusion: "It seems to me that nature's attempt to produce a thinking creature on this earth has failed."[8] Georg Picht, in listing the major world problems that science and technology can and must resolve, then asks: "How does science approach understanding (*Vernunft*)?"[9] And his reply is: understanding (*Vernunft*) is more than reason (*ratio*) and logic; it is responsible wisdom and insight. He instances the knowledge which in the language of faith is called "revelation"—a knowledge which we have hustled away. But science has become indifferent to *Vernunft* and *Unvernunft*—the "reasonable" and the "unreasonable".[10] All this one might sum up, perhaps, as follows: as a modern culture we have lost our identity and integrity. We do not want to be who we are.

6. *"Creatura"*. There is no ideological change, nor any "nature", that can produce a truly responsible human being who maintains his identity and integrity. According to the faith of Israel and the message of Christ, the Creator calls man out from "nature" in order to adopt him into the history of Salvation. For man today that means an operational choice from the possibilities offered by science and technology and a recognition of limits. Even the artificial world has to be included within this choice. We are "the experiment of God".[11] We owe something to God and our fellows. Man is *creatura*—and it is dangerous when the

[8] Max Born, *Die Zeit* 7–6–1968, cf. Georg Picht, *loc. cit.*, p. 143.

[9] Georg Picht, *loc. cit.*, pp. 131–42.

[10] Georg Picht, "Was heiszt aufgeklärtes Denken?", in *Zs. evang. Ethik*, no. 4 (1967).

[11] E. Rosenstock-Huessy, *Der Atem des Geistes* (Frankfurt), Essay: "Liturgisches Denken o. der Sieg ü. Renaissance u. Gegenreformation", p. 254.

churches' liturgies speak of the *naturalia* as a kind of solid bloc—*creatura along with* the entirety of things, plants animals and structures. We are all from and through and to God (Romans 11. 36). And every man is unique, once-for-all, after the image of God, the One and the Unique. Each man is an *"individuum ineffabile"*,[12] called to fellowship with God and his fellow men in history. History is an implementation of the creation,[13] as creation is itself history through the Word of God. In history man acquires a future, deliverance, prospect, he learns to give thanks and to respond. God gives him identity as a creature and sets him within a totality. After the Jewish prophets Christ showed us the way into this fundamental unity of *creatura* in a Whole of Salvation, History and Future. He has called us to share his work, to be a race of priests; and he who has himself done all that he owed it to God and his fellows to do, sends his apostles out to heal. E. Heimann,[14] discussing the tragedy of industrial society, is right, I think, to envisage science and technology in the light of this mandate to heal, to tend and to produce an abundance for human beings (Luke 9. 2; John 10. 11). Now at last man knows that hunger, disease and premature death need not be. But the principal task, to proclaim the kingdom of God, we have forgotten—forgotten how to locate it in the Whole and the Future. Our confused utterance and our refusal of responsibility for one another are grounded in a refusal to be *creatura*, that union between people and things that have a future. Our pride, inertia and falsehood stand in the way of historical progress. Our liturgy is "to rule", not "to serve"; and we lose our identity. God is our Salvation—Buber invariably renders this as Liberator. We are not *en route* for liberation. We forget. We go from prison to prison within anti-history: destruction, *status quo*, the natural activities that "go without saying" but cannot stand up to scientific criticism and to God's Word, but which we maintain in bewildering ideology, whether expressed or not, and which bar us from moving forward, deter us from our "exodus" from "nature". We do not give thanks. Rosenstock says: "Before we can think, it is our obligation to

[12] Leo Beck, *Individuum ineffabile* (Eranos-Vortrag, 1947).
[13] E. Heimann, *Theologie der Geschichte* (Kreuz-Verlag, 1966).
[14] E. Heimann, *loc. cit.*, Appendix, pp. 201–21.

give thanks."[15] We lose the capacity to speak because we disclaim the *creatura* in the conjunction of man with thing.

7. *The Word of God*. The real Liturgy, according to Hebrews 8. 2, is taking place in heaven, the (for us) unmanipulable part of creation; and that is the crucial thing. There the Consummation, the Kingdom of God as a visible Kingdom, is prepared and created. On earth the lesser liturgy is put in the hands of us human beings as co-workers, a "nation of priests"—what a sharing of control! "Only the man who lives his life as an office can be truly employed in living."[16] But what is it that guides and directs him? Theology and the Church will point to the Word of God in its three aspects: Jesus Christ, the incarnate Word, the Scriptures, proclamation. Yet only rarely, here and there, do we hear it openly being said that "Christian thinking does not have at its disposal a philosophy universal and concrete enough to encounter sciences and world views, social schemes and philosophies of culture on a footing of equality, let alone of superiority".[17] This is a basic point. Science one may regard as an ever expanding manual for decoding the cryptograms of a silent "nature". But the Church and the world have no code-book for the Word of God! For the Christian liturgy it is absolutely necessary that we be explicitly aware of this. What it means is that (a) God, who not only *has* spoken but is also speaking today, reserves the task of decoding to himself and himself attends with his Word upon each and every believer—a fellowship, a walking with God (Micah 6. 8; Romans 12. 2, what is good, acceptable and perfect); (b) this commits the believer, in addition to the intercourse he has with the Scriptures, to persistent listening and observing in the here and now, the context of present events, which will involve tuning his unique receiving apparatus in to the unique Transmitter; (c) the need for, and wonder of, Church and congregation. In the context of what is actually going on it must be alert, as a community of unique receivers of the Word, but should never lord it over the individual; for it is quite conceivable that an individual may receive a Word from the heavenly Liturgy. All anonymity must be excluded in a reciprocal exposure, with-

[15] E. Rosenstock-Huessy, *loc. cit.*, pp. 263 f.
[16] E. Rosenstock-Huessy, *Europäische Revolutionen* (1951), p. 557.
[17] J. M. de Jong, *Voorrang aan de toekomst* (1969), p. 179.

out which any exposing of the works of darkness cannot possibly succeed (Ephesians 5. 11).

The "self-utterance of God" (*Selbstwort Gottes*)[18] is more than the three persons, it embraces and proceeds from the heavenly Liturgy—the Spirit accompanies and interprets the Word to the believer in the state of alertness engendered in him by the three persons. The Word of God is *the* Creativity which makes new and makes relevant and up to date and yet—in perfect Identity—is the Same, in present, past and future. As compared with the most sensitive instruments known to science, man is the sole instrument in creation and in our artificial world sensitive enough to hear and register the Word. We can keep the Word as it addresses us—Mary kept all these sayings in her heart (Luke 2. 19)—or as with a technical computer we can erase it, obliterate it. Word, Spirit and happening (history) go together—Mary said: "may it happen to me according to your Word" (Luke 1. 38). Word and Spirit create their own channels, not super-"natural" but *in* "nature", which after all is God's creation. We cannot think fundamentally enough and subtly enough about the Word.[19] I prefer to use the term "Word/Spirit-field", by analogy with, for instance, theories of the field of formal potential in physics. There the receptor has a counter-effect on the transmitter. So too in the Word/Spirit-field: "there is knowledge in the Most High" (Psalm 73. 11). Our unuttered prayer, which always carries us into the totality, is heard by the Lord. The Word/Spirit-field in the course of events, of history, has a varying degree of "closeness": where God is active and wishes us to be present, there his Word is best received and interpreted. We have to tune in very accurately, admonished by the Scriptures, put in remembrance and in a posture of expectation by the message proclaimed, established by Jesus Christ in confident readiness for discipleship—and then Word and Spirit gather all this together in the form of commandment and of promise and write it, brand it upon our brain and nervous system ("our heart").[20]

[18] K. Barth, *Kirchliche Dogmatik* I–1 (Kaiser Verlag, Munich).

[19] It is the extremes that impress me: the very ass-like reaction of Balaam's ass in Numbers 22. 23, and the outpouring of the Holy Spirit at Pentecost: "How is it that we hear, each of us in his own native language?" (Acts 2. 8).

[20] Cf. Norbert Wiener, *God and Golem Inc.* (M.I.T. Press, 1964); see

Then we have to make the Word become flesh, incarnate it, in our history, it must be done, as a witness. It is the reception of this Word/Spirit-field which shows that man is no machine. The most refined computer cannot understand the Word. Our thinking, our reason, our logic are activated as purposive functions and brought to life by the Word. Thinking through thanking.

9. *Creaturely-creative*. The Word determines the limits of our logic, knocks a "hole" in logic where, independently of any logical inference, a new initiative, a breakthrough in the structures of thought occurs which is not irrational but supra-rational. It is at this hole, this channel, that we have to listen and *respond*. But the Word/Spirit-field is for all; unbelievers too can and will *reverberate*, not answering to the Creator and yet accomplishing his will. Here, amid the known and the familiar, the unknown and logically indeducible springs into history, and man is led to act freely in his "exodus" from "nature" and from anti-history, to act "in correspondence to the activity of God".[21] God is Creator: that is to say, man is all the time being called to act responsibly as both creaturely and creative being, to be creative in a way that does not abrogate his creatureliness and does not become an attribute, but does impel him to part company with every programmed mode of life, to break free of determinateness and extrapolation of "trends" in every form, and of all the frozen patterns of tradition, "self-evident" assumption and anti-history, also enslavement to ideology. Then something new can happen, a new turn of events.[22]

Both creaturely and creative, in accord with the heavenly Liturgy—this we are only in the warranted activity of love, charitableness, solidarity and humanity, in the Saving Dispensation. "For just so long as in all his researches and experiments the scientist fails to be as equally and as automatically concerned with the human aspect as he is with unimpeachable standards of technical performance, no real good is to be expected of science. It all turns upon a change of disposition, an altered state of

---

his views on the advantages offered by the compactness of our brains, pp. 72–3.

[21] Karl Barth, *Kirchliche Dogmatik*, III–4, p. 543: "in einer Entsprechung zum Tun Gottes".

[22] Cf. C. J. Dippel, "Creativiteit en natuurwetenschap", in *Geloof en Wetenschap* 66 (1968), pp. 201–18; *id*., 65 (1967), pp. 165–83.

mind."[23] *Mutatis mutandis*, what von Weizsäcker says here with regard to scientific experiment applies also to the technician, the business man, the economist. God wants people who acknowledge, honour and rejoice one another, are truly part and parcel of that total process whereby we are humanized and liberated. He wants a congregation that will be a training ground and vanguard, *in* the world, in a new liturgy which is a fresh affirmation, at all times, of the Christian community.[24]

[23] C. F. von Weizsäcker, *Zum Weltbild der Physik* (1958, 7th edn.), p. 182.
[24] Karl Barth, *Kirchliche Dogmatik*, III–4, p. 569.

Translated by Hubert Hoskins

Jörg Splett

Sacral—Profane—the Holy: Philosophical Considerations

I. Christian Desacralization

IN THE Bulletin of *Concilium* 9/2 (November 1966) American edn., Vol. 19) Father C. J. Geffré has concerned himself with the problem: "How far does the process of desacralization that is going on in the modern world serve what is truly sacred in our faith, that is, holiness? . . . Should we oppose this movement of desacralization, and re-create sacred regions in which the faith of modern man can take root?"[1] Father Geffré bases himself primarily upon the two opposed works of M. D. Chenu and J. Daniélou, but to these an impressive series of publications might be added. For the sake of simplicity, however, we shall be referring here primarily to the expositions of Geffré himself.

On the actual fact of desacralization, therefore, there seems to be a wide measure of agreement. Differences arise only with regard to the interpretation of this fact. Now, even if it is true that this lack of agreement is an indication of the ambiguity of the term "sacral" (Geffré), still ought we not perhaps to regard it as having further implications too, bearing upon the actual *fact* of desacralization?

There is an influential thesis to the effect that desacralization is a sign and a function of the Christian faith in the process of realizing its true nature (Gogarten, Metz, Chenu, etc.). Against this U. Mann has presented in summary form seven objections[2]

[1] C. J. Geffré, "The Tension between Desacralization and Spirituality", *Concilium* 9/2 (1966), p. 57 (American edn., vol. 19).

[2] U. Mann, *Das Christentum als absolute Religion* (Darmstadt, 1970), pp. 74–77.

which may here be set forth as follows (formulated in our own terms):

1. Would it not be true to say that desacralization springs not so much from the Gospel as from the natural sciences of the modern age? Indeed has not this movement been due precisely to the fact that when confronted with the challenge of natural science the Church introduced the cleavage between the researches of natural science on the one hand and religious, moral and metaphysical questions on the other? In other words, faced with findings of philosophical or medical science which were unassailable she "relegated research to the realm of the profane" (with the consequence that today rules for interpreting the findings of research and for conducting scientific research in a responsible way have had to be devised, as it were, as an afterthought).

2. Had it not been for natural science would not the accustomed way of using the gospel message have continued unchanged for a very long time before a way was found—and, furthermore, as the outcome of a mistaken attitude on the part of the Church—of breaking fresh ground and finding a new approach?

3 and 4. Was the world of classical antiquity really so very "sacral"? Did it not recognize any spheres which were basically emancipated from all religious connections (the obscure theme of Gnosis!)? Did it not, on the other hand, consciously and deliberately pursue the aim of shaping the world according to its own will? (We may, for instance, compare the plans of cities and maps of streets of classical antiquity with those of the Middle Ages.)

5. Did not the new awakening of the Renaissance and the new humanism consciously attach itself to classical antiquity precisely as opposed to Christianity?

6. How far was the success of Christianity in its early days based upon the fact that it coincided with the quest for religion which arose from the desacralizing process of later classical times? At that time the power of this new movement was sufficient to bind the "focal points of secular interest" to the sacral,

and they were only liberated once more when its hold upon them was relaxed.

7. Do not periods of desacralization necessarily arise from time to time throughout the whole of the history of religions (e.g., the First Intermediate Period in ancient Egypt, the "Homeric rationalism", the period of the Greek philosophers, the Karma teaching of ancient India)? And surely we should think above all of the study of medicine in all cultures. We should not be too hasty in interpreting as belonging to the sphere of sacral magic a rational approach which deviates from our own.

This brings us to the eighth point, the assumption that religion can never be totally obliterated but at most—for a time—suppressed. The element of the sacral can only be "thrust into the background" as, for instance, when from being expressed in external symbols it is relegated to the sphere of the unconscious (incidentally, perhaps this may account for the increase in our own times in neuroses and psychoses). This assumption agrees with the findings of Geffré when he points to compensating phenomena which he regards as signs of a *re*sacralizing process.

We do not intend here to discuss these objections. U. Mann has deliberately presented them not as counter-theories (to negate the theory that has been put forward) but as counter-*questions* (to restrict its application). We may begin, rather, by pointing out a further idea which, to a certain extent, confirms their general tendency from the opposite direction: if we admit that the desacralizing process derives from the Jewish and Christian revelation of God as Creator and of Jesus in his humanity as the Son of God, was this process therefore the only (legitimate) outcome of a message of this kind?

Every sense of the numinous known to classical antiquity pales into insignificance beside the awareness of divinity as immanent in a world which comes wholly from the hand of God and remains wholly in his hand. Precisely to the extent that in this world there are no taboos, that nothing is withheld, since it is handed over in its entirety to man, this world is and will be *given* to him (and he himself together with it). A gift is meant to be, and certainly must be, accepted, but precisely as a gift. In other words it must not simply be "taken over", but received in thankfulness and conscious appreciation: with our eyes upon the giver and in an attitude of trust towards him. If a message of this kind has a liberating effect, then it liberates us not, properly speaking, for work but for praise. It gives space and time for contemplation and glorification. Science ("to know in order to foresee in order to be able") is not needed here. That is why Israel—differing in this from the great empires and from Greece with their polytheism—never in fact developed any science.

This idea too is put forward merely as a question, not as a thesis. In it, therefore, a world order is conceived which involves a seven-day week with Sunday as the climax (the Sabbath is indeed for man in order that he may realize his true nature by being with God and for him in worship and recreation), whereas the manifestos in which other theories are expressed sometimes read as though in the institution of Sunday (considered as *dies dominica*) we are dealing with "a remnant of magic" carried over from the religious attitudes of paganism. But on both theories the distinction between Sunday and working days appears as an evil, whether it is interpreted as a sign of a desacralization process which is unfortunately growing or alternatively as a sign of a still surviving preoccupation with the sacred.[3]

II. Sacral—Profane

It will be realized that the relationship between the sacral and the profane needs to be defined more precisely. For the liturgist the most serviceable definition of the sacral may be one which defines it in terms of the intrinsic relationship which it bears (both of its nature and in its function) to the cult.[4] But to the philosopher it is precisely the implied separation involved in this

[3] See e.g. G. W. F. Hegel, *Begriff der Religion, ed. Lasson* (Hamburg, 1966), p. 11. In his philosophy of religion he seeks to bridge this gulf precisely by pointing to an alleged Christian origin of the concept of "worldliness" and "the earth as the this-worldly sphere") (*Philosophie der Weltgeschichte*, ed. Lasson (Hamburg, 1968), pp. 876, 747); cf. W. Kern, "Atheismus—Christentum—emanzipierte Gesellschaft", *Zeitschrift für katholische Theologie* 91 (1969), pp. 289–321.

[4] Cf. C. v. Korvin-Krasinski, "Untergang des Sakralan?", *Liturgie und Münchtum*, Heft 41 (Maria Laach, 1967) pp. 11–32. J. Pieper, "Sakralität und 'Entsakralisierung' ", *Hochland* 61 (1969), pp. 481–496, quoted (p. 487); Thomas Aquinas, *S.Th.* II–II 99, 1: *Sacrum dicitur aliquid ex eo, quod ad divinum cultum ordinatur.*

definition that appears problematical. On the other hand to speak of an "original sacredness" which "by virtue of the mystery of creation" is "coextensive with the truth that is in the world by the sheer force of what it is in itself" (Geffré) seems to rule out any real separation at all.

C. Geffré adduces a little book of J. Grand'Maison's which is, in fact, extremely illuminating, *Le monde et le sacré*.[5] According to this author "the sacral is not a thing in itself like the profane (or better the earthly), but an objective relation that is coextensive with being and present in every mode of being and every reality". How then can Grand'Maison go on to say: "It must be so constituted that it stands apart from the profane yet at the same time summons it to be consecrated"? Surely we should not call this state of being transcendentally related which is present in all created things the sacral—not even the "original sacral". Rather it is the condition which makes sacralization possible. Nor is this state the holy but rather the ontological manifestation of this (J. G. Fichte), its unfolding (Nicholas of Cusa), we might say, its worldly dimension.[6] If we are to express this condition in terms of the world and its reality it is the *holiness* of these in the sense of the moral directive: "We must hold sacred the rights or the dignity of the person". The appropriate attitude towards this holiness latent in the creaturely, therefore, is *attentiveness* (using the term with its full Kantian force).

Of its very nature, then, the sacral is in a state of being related to other being. But on any adequate definition of the sacral a further dimension must be included as pertaining to this connatural state, that namely of time and history. What we are concerned with, therefore, is the fact that at certain points in history "holiness" becomes an "object of attention" precisely *as* such—not indeed as the subject of (philosophical or theological) reflection (i.e., into the nature of what it is), but as an event in human life, something that we come across as a matter of concrete experience. Then a *further* stage follows in which this occurrence is also systematically reflected upon, but above all

[5] J. Grand'Maison, *Le monde et le sacré*, I. *Le sacré* (Paris 1966), p. 26.

[6] See J. Splett, *Sakrament der Wirklichkeit*, Vorüberlegungen zu einem weltlichen Begriff des Heiligen (Würzburg, 1968). Cf. *idem*, "Symbol in the Encyclopedia of Theology, *Sacramentum Mundi*.

man responds to this occurrence by proclaiming it and acting upon it in myth and cult.

A given place or time, in so far as they constitute the "point of contact" for such an event (a tree or bush, a mountain, a stone...) thereby become "something special", set apart in that sense which is neither moral nor aesthetic but precisely indicative of a unique quality, and which is expressed by the term "sacral". Thus the response of the cult to the sacral is prior to the relationship of the sacral to the cult. It is only by responding to the sacral that the cult is constituted as what it truly is and that the places and times, acts and participants, documents and vessels belonging to it acquire a sacral character. (This sacral character is, in a certain sense, to be considered secondary, though this does not exclude the possibility that within it certain "primary" epiphanies or manifestations of the holy may also occur again and again.)

Now it is only as a correlative of the sacral as defined here (whether primary or secondary), and only in virtue of its prior existence, that there is such a thing as the profane, precisely because the event of the sacral has already taken place. Not merely "sacral" but "profane" as well, therefore, is shown to be the expression of a relation. The profane is not profane in itself and of its very nature, but simply that which it can be, should be and is, at any given point in virtue of being a "reality belonging to this earth" (this is why desacralization could, in a certain sense, just as well or even better be called deprofanization or, to express the same thing in positive terms, as several authors actually do in order to avoid any pejorative connotations, secularization, "the attribution of 'this-worldly' status").

Relation implies distinction between the two related things, but precisely in so far as they are connected. Let us begin by considering the relationship of the sacral (as the determining factor) to the profane. (1) Simply in virtue of what it is in itself it makes the profane to be the non-sacral. It does this without devaluing it, but still unmistakably. (2) The sacral is *ipso facto* related to the profane (and the profane to it), but at the same time the term implies that that holiness which is proper to all that is has been made a theme for investigation. Nevertheless, the manner in which it is related to the profane is not such that it draws it within its own orbit. On the contrary, it establishes the line of demarcation between itself and the profane and is in contact with it, so to say, "by proxy".

Of course it is not the sacral itself that establishes this kind of relationship but rather that which is manifested as belonging to the sacral together with him who experiences it. It is these that establish the relationship between the sacral and the non-sacral. It is established through *freedom*. Hence the misuses of human freedom are revealed in the concrete forms in which this relationship is expressed. These wrong forms destroy the image and meaning of the sacral and thereby of the profane as well, and arouse corresponding reactions. There is, for example, a tendency for that which belongs to the world to be absorbed into the secondary or tertiary degrees of sacralization (i.e., where that which is sacral in a secondary sense has subsequently been speculated upon and made a subject of theorizing). Against this tendency the process of "secularization" is a salutary one both for the world and for the sacral itself. But even (and precisely) in its undistorted form the claim of the sacral provokes (Scripture says "tempts") us to react to it in such a way as to maintain that we can take over what Grand'Maison has to say concerning the "autonomy" of the profane. And then, in the *"incurvatio super seipsum"* involved in this we already find what could be called, from the viewpoint of faith, "the cult of the profane" or what has been called "the world" by John and "secularism" by Gogarten.

The various erroneous forms, therefore (each of which would require a separate explanation), might provide a starting-point for working out the various meanings attached to the terms "sacral" and "profane". The more precise distinctions which would thus be arrived at would then serve to throw light upon one part of the controversy about the problems with which we are here concerned. In this the very fact of the alleged secularization which is taking place today would be called in question (in other words its extent), let alone the question of whether it has a Christian significance. In other words the following questions would be raised: (1) How far the removal of the Church's influence necessarily signifies a desacralization. (2) How far both of these factors (as distinct from the disappearance of specific modes of the sacral) are particularly characteristic of our times.[7]

It must be admitted that the removal of misconceptions (to the extent that this is possible) has the effect of throwing still more sharply into relief the oppositions which exist between the various ways of understanding something which is, of its nature, unambiguously single in meaning: particular sets of circumstances, wider developments as these affect our idea of the sacral, the Christian, the holy—indeed of being and of significance as such. Here, finally, different plans for the world make their appearance, deriving not merely from the basic decisions of individuals (or groups) but from an actual *call* which they feel they have received at some particular point. It is not enough to say that the one who experiences the sacral relates it to his world or interprets it. Rather he is actually involved in, and deeply affected in his own personal life by that which is manifested to him as belonging to it. The sacral is sacred neither in virtue of what it is in itself nor in contradistinction to the profane, but because of the holy which shines forth in it.

III. The Holy

We have called the element of holiness inherent in that which pertains to this world the "worldly aspect" of the holy, its manifestation (considered as the "term" of the process by which it comes to be manifested, just as creation as embodied in the *creatura* is the "term" of the act of creation considered as *creatio*). We have defined the sacral as the "expression in thematic form" (the manifestation) of this act of being manifested. From both points of view, therefore, we have now to inquire into the nature of that which is manifested.

With regard to the discussion of the holy K. Löwith has remarked that the element in it which so fascinates us is "the religious motif. It is true that this has become emancipated from the Christian faith. But in virtue of the very indeterminacy arising from this, its freedom from the fetters of dogma, its claims

[7] See J. Matthes, *Religion und Gesellschaft* and also *Kirche und Gessellschaft, Einführung in die Religionssoziologie* I–II, Rowohlts deutsche enzyklopädie 279/280 and 312/313 (Reinbek, 1967 and 1969).

are all the stronger upon those who are no longer believing Christians but would still like to be religious."[8] Is the discussion of the holy, therefore, in fact a discussion about God which only lacks the courage to acknowledge itself as such? Certainly this kind of discussion does exist also. But in its true and ultimate significance something else is being pointed to here. What is in question is no mere vague religiosity, but the designation of that unique quality of being absolute and unconditioned which purely ethical categories are quite inadequate to express.

C. Geffré considers, against Dumoulin, that purely ethical categories are closer to the Christian idea of the sacral than to the pagan one. Without entering into this discussion (except to say that surely we should not be so hasty to designate the pagan idea of the sacral as "magical") we may recall P. Tillich's position. With reference to the practice of Catholics this author emphasizes that personal holiness signifies not religious or moral perfection but a state of transparency to the absolute basis of being. In this connection he has pointed out a twofold danger. On the one hand, if we understand the holy too much in terms of the numinous or even the demonic we may obscure its divinity by eliminating the element of the pure. On the other hand, however, if we identify the holy too much with the pure we may draw it down to the level of the merely secular rules of morality, and deprive it of the depths of the mystery which it involves.[9]

Certainly—to take up the question with which this study was introduced—there can be no question of "creating new spheres of the sacral (as though one could 'make' anything of this kind) in order that the faith of modern man can take root". The revelation of the sovereign and personal God does not need any specifically religious *a priori*, and faith is not the activation of any such *a priori* disposition, but rather the state in which revelation has "arrived at its goal". But we can ask ourselves whether such a manifestation of itself and its acceptance on the part of the subject do not necessarily constitute the state of the sacral. We must avoid restricting ourselves rigidly to certain specific forms

[8] K. Löwith, *Heidegger—Denker in dürftiger Zeit*, 3rd ed. (Göttingen, 1965), p. 111.

[9] P. Tillich, *Systematic Theology* I (Chicago, Illinois, 1951), pp. 146 f and 253.

of the sacral (just as we must avoid accepting only certain specific styles as art and so having to condemn any new forms as anti-artistic or "non-art"). However true it may be, therefore, that the goal of this history is the eternal festival in the city without a temple, however true it may be that the cleavage represented by the rending of the temple veil signifies the beginning of this final consummation, still, even allowing for this, the fact that the difference between the dimensions of the sacral and the profane still survives must not be regarded as *in itself* a negative factor. For this is the sole way in which history can be brought to this, its due and final consummation. Different relationships (to the world, to the "thou", to God) freely entered into cannot immediately become themes for investigation. First we have to achieve that ultimate perspective in which they are all integrated. (Moreover, it is not simply we but the holy itself as well which determines the "hour" of epiphany and festival.) The distinction between festivals and ordinary days is familiar in other contexts too, both in public and private life, in which various exercises of human freedom exist side by side. And here too this distinction should not be presented—with Buber—as a "depressed" alternative to the contrast between the world of "thou" and the world of "it".[10] Admittedly, in the form it actually assumes *in the concrete* this distinction is constantly characterized by the fact that our human circumstances are not conducive to salvation and are alienated from the holy.

In many ways those beings which are apprehensible to us in our everyday lives can be transformed and suddenly illumined from within—illumined in two distinct senses of the term. The accustomed supports fail. The "usual" loses its force as providing a firm basis, and yet at the same time a new order of being with a sustaining power of its own glimmers through the surface of things. It may be that today poets and artists bear witness to this more freely (even though often they are quite unaccustomed to it) than the theologians.

The modes in which this experience takes place cannot now be discussed. In any case, even from the philosophical standpoint, our reflections upon them would be inadequate if we sought to

[10] Cf. J. Splett, *Der Mensch in seiner Freiheit* (Mainz, 1967), esp. pp. 107 ff.; B. Casper, *Das dialogische Denken* (Freiburg, 1967), pp. 297 ff., 342 ff.

assign their unique quality to the realms of devotion and the cult, or to make a selection of them according to our own tastes, using them as a starting-point for some rational pursuit of our own. Mere phenomenology is inadequate to do justice to the degree of importance and the reality of what is encountered (the more so since it would lead, ultimately speaking, to the psychology of religion). What is made manifest here has a rational content which it is the task of human *thought* to explore. But still it must be explored precisely as content. This means that in the process of arriving at our findings our speculations must conform to the holy precisely as holy. Through these speculations of ours, considered precisely as speculations (not only or primarily as adoration or religious meditation), and as speculations about the holy (not merely reflections upon the responses and reactions of religion to it) the holy must itself be allowed to be holy.[11]

The distinctive quality of this phenomenon that we encounter cannot, of course, be described any more than quality in general. Even Rudolph Otto could only take refuge in specially coined terms or in the "numinous quotation marks" so often deplored in order to direct his readers' attention to their own experience. As a first step, however, we might point (with Scheler) to the experience of salvation, i.e., to the fact that in this event the thought, the thinker, achieves harmony with himself and with the world, with being taken as a whole, precisely in that he commits himself to the event. And this in spite of—indeed precisely *in* the fact that in this experience he is utterly carried out of himself and "reduced to nothing" by the holy (in the Old Testament the tension involved here is expressed in such passages as: "no man can see me and still remain alive"—Ex. 33. 20; and "Show us thy countenance and we are saved"—Ps. 80 (79). 4, 20).

The holy is that significance which provides other things with meaning while itself remaining unfathomable. But this is still not precisely what it means to call it *holy*. Thus it only enters our field of vision at that point at which our mind forgets itself and its salvation to lose itself in the absolute and unconditional sove-

[11] Cf. B. Welte, *Auf der Spur des Ewigen* (Freiburg 1965), esp. pp. 315–336 (Der Gottesbeweis und die Phänomenologie der Religion); B. Casper, K. Hemmerle, P. Hünermann, *Besinnung auf das Heilige* (Freiburg, 1966).

reignty of that which is revealed. However many objections may be raised today against speaking of the holy, I could never devise any other word by which to call this absolute (i.e., transcending the limiting factor in all relationships) sublimity and glory (*"kabod"*, *"doxa"*) which men have again and again found it necessary to express by the image of light.

The holy is itself of itself and through itself and not in virtue of force but of "right". For this reason there is a demand that we should speak not of "the holy" but only of "him who is holy". Certainly such sheer sublimity and meaningfulness cannot be anything less than personal. But on the other hand even the concept of the personal can be applied to it only analogously, i.e., with "endless dissimilarities, however great the similarity may be". The impersonal way of speaking of it is intended to preserve this distinction. We have, in fact, also to avoid explaining it simply as a "quality"—one among many—belonging to the All-Highest (something like moral perfection). When we speak of the holy we signify God himself (in his decision to be "for us") as *the* Mystery.

Now precisely because of the inadequacy of all ways of speaking of it this would have to be discussed at length. Here, however, only a single closing reference must serve to indicate what is meant: Such ways of speaking are intended to perform in the dimension of thought what the liturgy of the Church expresses in the unfathomable depths of that verse of the *Gloria* which runs: "We give you thanks (not because you are our salvation but) for your great glory".

Translated by David Bourke

Juan Llopis

The Liturgy celebrates God's Presence in the World and his Invitation to Man

I. The Absence of God and the Need for him in the World of Today

ESTABLISHING the absence of God from the world of today has become a commonplace, as the proliferation of the "death of God" school of theological writing amply demonstrates. Yet various inquiries in different countries show that the contrary phenomenon also exists: people today are once again feeling the need for God; for many there is a sort of "resurrection of God".[1]

If the cultural fact of the "death of God" is essentially ambiguous, that of his "resurrection" is no less so from the Christian point of view, since the God who is being resurrected is very unlikely to be the "God of Abraham, Isaac and Jacob" or the "Father of our Lord Jesus Christ". At best he is likely to be the God of deism, and often enough modern man seems to experience a nostalgia for a mythical and magical God to give him the feeling of security that he cannot get from technological society, however great its material triumphs.

Faced with the contrasting situations of the absence of God and the religious need felt by many, Christians have an inescapable duty to bear witness to the living God, since "it is the task of the Church to make God the Father and his incarnate Son present and almost visible, while continually renewing and purifying itself under the guidance of the Holy Spirit".[2] The

[1] Cf. J. Duquesne, *Dieu pour l'homme d'aujourd'hui* (Paris, 1970), pp. 11–96.

[2] *Gaudium et Spes*, n. 21.

Church's specific mission is not to elaborate rational proofs of the existence of God and present them to men in the expectation of convincing them. No, without forgetting that the Christian must "be always ready to give reasons for his hope to anyone who asks him",[3] or that many difficulties in the way of the approach to faith are intellectual in character, it remains true that the witness of a living and mature faith is generally the best way of making God's presence in the world felt. As one writer has summed it up neatly: "The reply of the Church and the believer to the challenge of atheism can only be the counter-challenge of faith, serving love and historical efficacy".[4]

II. Liturgy Celebrates the Inviting Presence of God

The life of the Christian should be a witness to the presence of God in the world, and one of its most important aspects is liturgical action, through which "the principal manifestation of the Church is brought about".[5] The Christian has to be a living sign of the presence of God in the world in all his actions and all circumstances of his life, and the Church has to witness to God's saving actions in all its activities, but for both it is the liturgy that both makes this need more pressing and offers the greatest possibilities for its satisfaction.

The liturgy is the epiphany of the Church and so the epiphany of God. But the God thus shown forth in the liturgy is not the God of deism or the god of natural religiosity, but the God revealed in Jesus Christ, at once transcendent and immanent, the creator of the world and the final end of history, the inaccessible and unnamable Lord whom we can yet with all confidence call Father. In the first place, the means the liturgy uses to discover this God to us are not those of rational argument, moral precept or aesthetic intuition, but rather those of its proper genre: that of "religious celebration", which is so *sui generis* that it transcends the way of religion itself. In the second place, the end the liturgy proposes to us through these means is not a God considered directly in such a category as Supreme Truth, Infinite Good or

[3] Cf. 1 Pet. 3. 15.

[4] O. González de Cardenal, *Meditación teológica desde España* (Salamanca, 1970), p. 89.

[5] *Sacrosanctum Concilium*, n. 41.

Ineffable Beauty: its specific goal is the God who is totally Other yet has made himself flesh of our flesh, the transcendent God who in Christ became one of us.

To say that celebration is the specific instrument used by the liturgy is to assert the fact that liturgy is deeply rooted in human nature, since religious rituals have always been the best means for man to come vitally to grips with the basic mystery of his existence. But when we say that the God celebrated in our liturgy is the God revealed by Jesus Christ, this implies that we have to approach the liturgical rites in a rigorously critical spirit, if we are to make sure that they become effective signs of faith and not just a vague expression of religiosity.

The presence of God celebrated in the Christian liturgy is something more than just his "natural" presence in everything; it is more specifically his "historical" presence, which at its most characteristic takes the form of personal and loving invitations to men: God may rule over the destiny of his people, but he also speaks to their hearts. It is an "inviting presence", whose culmination is represented by the mission of the Son of God himself. In Christ, God's invitation is hypostatized to the utmost, manifested and made present not in words and signs, but in a visible humanity, a real person who can be touched, the "Word who is made flesh and comes to dwell amongst us".[6]

God's invitation through Christ finds its appropriate response in man's faith. Faith is born of hearing the evangelizing Word with its accompanying signs. Once accepted, faith needs doctrinal deepening and practical rooting. But these are not enough: like any encounter of love, faith needs very special means of expression, and what characterizes these is their gratuitousness and apparent uselessness. It is the task of liturgical celebration to supply this necessary dimension to the encounter of faith, the fruit of God's loving invitation and man's free response to it.

The liturgy has to show very clearly that the God it celebrates is not one who is there to be "used" for selfish ends, but one who should be "enjoyed" in the gratuitousness of love; not the "useful" God of deism, but the "useless" God of faith. The liturgy

[6] Jn 1. 14. Cf. J. Murphy-O'Connor, "The Presence of God through Christ in the Church and the World", in *Concilium* 10/5 (Dec. 1969) (American edn., vol. 50).

should also be admitted to be "useless", in that it "serves" no practical purpose. At the same time, it is absolutely necessary, in that without it Christians would lose sight of the gratuitous character of God's gift and of the essential freedom of faith. Exactly what this "gratuitousness" of the liturgy means as a necessary condition for its showing forth of the God of faith needs to be examined in greater detail.

III. The Gratuitousness of the Word and Signs

The liturgy has certain elements that can be called "objective". For the sake of simplicity these can be reduced to two: the Word and signs.

There are many different sorts of words used in the liturgical actions: the proclamation of the Word of God, sacramental formulas, prayers, hymns, acclamations, monitions, homily. But all liturgical forms of words are built up around two forms of dialogue: God's dialogue with his people,[7] and the dialogue of the members of the assembly among themselves.[8] In both forms, what is actually said is less important than what is intended to be signified: the loving, gratuitous encounter between God and his people.

"In the liturgy, the Word of God is not just announced, studied, analysed or simply read, as such, but *celebrated.* One cannot celebrate ideas, but only deeds. So the liturgy considers the Word of God as something that happens, as an event. What does happen? The basic event that takes place here and now is that God talks to his people: this is more important than what is said at this moment. The process of God communicating himself to humanity, with the Church has known and accepted through its faith, is now made present and real in the liturgical action. This is the object of the celebration: what is being celebrated is precisely God's presence to the assembly *through the communication* of his Word."[9] Any intent to "use" the Word of God impedes the absolute gratuitousness of the divine gift and

[7] *Sacrosanctum Concilium*, n. 33.

[8] Cf. *Institutio generalis Missalis Romani*, n. 14.

[9] J. Camps, "La Palabra de Dios es celebrada", in *Phase* 10 (1970), pp. 145 ff.

embargoes the primacy of God's initiative in the work of salvation.

It must also be borne in mind that the only way for liturgical celebration to be a loving "dialogue" between God and his people is through the authentically human quality of the dialogue of the members of the assembly among themselves. Communication between God and man uses the channels of human dialogue, and these have to be kept absolutely clear if they are not to provide an obstacle to the personal meeting with God. Liturgy is a celebration of the dialogue between God and man to the extent that all its words are words of dialogue. Any distortion of its dialogue structure involves a compromise of its meaning and efficacy. But when the gift of the Word of God is celebrated with joy, and liturgical gatherings take on an atmosphere of dialogue, then they become the best demonstration of the fact that the God of faith does not primarily seek to impose acceptance of a "doctrine" on us, but graciously to draw us across the threshold of his intimacy.

Like all celebration, the liturgy contains typical means of expression, which can be called "festive actions" or "signs". Every liturgical sign is at once a human gesture making use of natural elements and an anamnesic imitation of divine gestures, since it is a re-enactment of a loving gesture of Christ. From this it follows that any falsity in the human gesture or in its link with the history of salvation devalues the significative and operative force of the signs. Then, instead of the gleaming transparencies through which the presence of God in Christ can shine that they should be, they turn into opaque screens shutting men off from their personal encounter with God.

In this whole complex constellation of liturgical signs, however, it should be borne in mind that the most important element is not so much their logical transparency as their "poetic" expressiveness, in its double function of symbolic reference and creative bringing about. What these signs do is not so much to "say" something as to "suggest" and "operate". They suggest a dimension of reality that lies beyond the realm of simple rational truth, and they operate a contact with the inviting presence of God, on its level of gratuitous and loving gift. Hence the need for liturgical signs to appear as gratuitous and festive actions rather than as numbers in a code of communication, for them to try to demonstrate the ineffable nature of the encounter of faith and to bring it about in its deepest fullness.

Any completed sign possesses a noetic dimension, with which it carries out its advisory and informative functions, but also a poetic or operative dimension, consisting in orientating the active response of the receiver and producing union between him and the emitter of the sign. A liturgical sign is certainly a call to attention and a revelation of a message, and so has to be intelligible and transparent, but it is above all an invitation and a meeting-place, and so must be attractive and multi-functional. The pragmatic dimension of liturgical signs is of far greater importance than their semantic function, but this does not mean that their end is simply utilitarian: what they express and bring about is as gratuitous as the meaning behind presents and gestures of love—the interpersonal encounter born of free and loving invitation and acceptance. For the Christian, liturgical rites are not mere teaching instruments designed to foster a better understanding of the meaning of God's revelation, nor utilitarian means of appropriating its force; they are, above all and before all, lyrical explosions of his faith, playful and gratuitous shows of his love, shouts and songs of admiration and hope, through which all can come to know that the God of Christian faith is not the theoretical God of the philosophers, or the "usable" God of religion, but the "God and Father of our Lord Jesus Christ, who in Christ has blessed us with every spiritual blessing . . . and sealed us with the seal of the promised Holy Spirit".[10] It is the very gratuitousness of the liturgical signs that constitutes the guarantee of the sincerity of our relationship with God and the quality of the divine image we should offer to the world. Our relationship to God and our capacity for evangelizing will be measured according to the specific weight of our "feasts", in which liberty and love will be put to the test.

IV. Free and Eucharistic Liturgical Assemblies

If gratuitousness is the necessary condition for the objective elements in the liturgy to achieve their objective, it is no less so

[10] Eph. 1. 3, 13.

for the "subjective" element—the liturgical community or assembly. The liturgy will be a true celebration when it is performed by gratuitous assemblies: that is, assemblies made up of free and eucharistic beings, Christians who come together through the impulse of the force of faith and love alone, motivated principally by a desire to praise and give thanks.

The liturgical assembly is a sign of the inner freedom of the members of the people of God. Liturgy forces one to waste time and to make use of material things to no utilitarian purpose. Not that the Christian despises earthly things: he is just not slavishly tied to them. He makes use of things and serves other men, but always in the spirit of a free child of God. The clearest sign of this dominion over things is to know how to do without them when needs be for the sake of devoting oneself purely to praising God and living in harmony with one's brothers. The Christian may waste time and material things, but he knows that this waste is the guarantee of his lordly freedom.

So he will not seek to cut down the time spent in prayer, will not count the costs of his worship, will not act like a businessman in his dealings with God and his brethren, seeking the greatest gain for the least expenditure. He will, on the contrary, give generously of his time and money to the, humanly speaking, non-productive work of serving God in prayer, giving thanks and praise, and to celebrating together with his fellows. So the Sunday eucharist is the overt sign of the Christian's sovereign freedom from all slaveries. To be able to spend an hour in the service of God and reunion with his brothers is the proof that he has learned to enjoy freedom. But if it is just a burdensome obligation, fulfilled with reluctance, then instead of a sign of freedom, it becomes a chain of slavery and a deadly counter-sign for believers and unbelievers alike.

A eucharistic attitude is a basic prerequisite for an assembly that comes together freely for liturgical celebration. The action of giving thanks has a two-way outlook: first, we look to ourselves, and instead of concentrating on our misfortunes, we take stock of the wonders that God has worked in us; then, we look towards the author of our glory, praising him in admiration and giving him thanks with joy. In this way, our giving thanks goes beyond a simple show of gratitude: although it is based on the favours we have received at God's hands, it merges with pure and disinterested praise. So we do not just say, "We give you thanks for the favours you have shown us", but, "We give you thanks for your great glory".

The eucharist is the greatest expression of the Christian's inner freedom, and the supreme manifestation of his love for God and his brothers. Christians contribute to demonstrating that the God of faith is the God of freedom to the extent that they overcome the natural tendency to centre prayer on self-interested petitions and give themselves over to disinterested praise. They co-operate in the effectiveness of the Christian liturgy, as an epiphany of divine love itself, to the extent that they open themselves to others to enable them to discover the wonder of God's love.

Freedom, love, thanksgiving: these three traditionally linked aspects of the Christian eucharist must be retained in their full vigour today if our liturgical assemblies are really to act as living signs of God's presence and his invitation to mankind. It is significant that in all rites the great eucharistic prayer, the centre of the liturgy and of the life of the Church, is preceded by a dialogue between the president and the people, through which the members of the assembly are "invited" to join in the giving of thanks. This is an invitation appealing to their love and freedom, not a juridical obligation weighing on their consciences.

What they are being invited to do is to give thanks to the Father, and to share the bread and wine in brotherly love, as signs of Christ's loving self-abandonment to the will of God and the service of his fellow men. Yet what we have generally had is an insistence on the obligatory aspect of the Mass, a lack of understanding of the content of the great eucharistic prayer, and a disconnection between sacramental communion and life in union with the brethren. We need look no further for the main reasons for the scant influence the liturgical assembly has had on Christian life for so many years, and for the deformed image of God and our faith it has presented to the eyes of the world. So it is vital for us to rediscover the way of freedom, of disinterest and love, that will bring us back to the free brotherly eucharists that the world today has such need to see.

V. Continuous Purification of the Liturgy

The way is not easy and is studded with obstacles and difficulties. The very nature of liturgical activities lends itself to two dangerous tendencies that can drastically compromise the authentic manifestation of pure faith: *ritualism*, which gives greater weight to gesture and formula than to inner disposition, and *angelism*, which unilaterally stresses the disinterested orientation of the liturgy, with consequent alienation and escapism. We have to fight against both these deviations, using, if necessary, the growing process of secularization, which is an effective antidote to their dangers.[11]

The Christian liturgy has suffered flesh wounds resulting from unwarranted relapse into religious ways that faith should have abolished or purified. Instead of being a genuine expression of faith through admiring adoration and grateful praise, it has often turned into superstition or magic, an expression of servile fear of God or an arrogant pretension to laying hold of his favours. The secular outcry against religious ritualism is undoubtedly contributing to the awakening of the Christian conscience on this point, and is accelerating the process of expugning ritualist excesses from the heart of the Christian liturgy. The secular attack on outward religious forms is forcing the liturgy farther and farther back on to its own ground, shedding inferior forms of religiosity as it goes and seeking manifestations of faith that will have something to say to men of today. Far from being a loss, this represents an enormous gain for the purity of the liturgy.

There is also the danger of exaggerated spiritualism. By stressing the gratuitousness of the liturgy, this has induced the faithful to make use of liturgical acts as a means of evading their responsibilities in the world. Now, the demand for realism, energetically pressed by the secular mentality, is having its effect on more alert Christians and forcing them to adopt a more human and responsible attitude to the liturgy. Liturgy should not be a means of escaping from the world, but of serving it better. The minutes devoted to worship and prayer, despite their intrinsic gratuitousness, are not minutes wasted, but tremendously effective with

[11] Cf. L. Maldonado, *Secularización de la liturgia* (Madrid, 1970), pp. 185–202.

regard to the responsibilities of believers in the world. Liturgical life does not consist in having one's head in the clouds, but in putting oneself in contact with the saving power of Christ and so in a position to fight shoulder-to-shoulder with other men for a juster, freer and more habitable world.

Thus stripped of ritualism and angelism, the liturgy will contribute to the formation of Christian communities that will know how to be present in the world and to be an expressive sign of the presence of God, how to communicate with all men and to make their meeting for worship a brotherly meeting, full of communication and dialogue, through which its members will arrive at a personal encounter with God and be heralds of the Father's loving invitation to the whole world.[12] It will then become fully true that the liturgy celebrates God's presence in the world and his invitation to man.

[12] Cf. J. Robert, "Présence et Parole", in *Parole et Mission* 49 (1970), pp. 158–66.

Translated by Paul Burns

PART II
DOCUMENTATION CONCILIUM

Evert de Jong

Liturgical Developments in Holland

IT IS very difficult to provide a survey of the various liturgical experiments which are being tried out at present in the Church in Holland. The widely divergent celebrations and the great variety in which they are given shape not only make it impossible to cover all but also to pick out what is representative of all that happens in the liturgical services in so many places, either privately or publicly.

There is no solid documentation and such a documentation can only be built up with the co-operation of all concerned. Perhaps the new Liturgical Commission set up by the Dutch bishops will do something about this.

In general one can say that there is widespread liturgical activity everywhere and that in any parish the laity sooner or later take the initiative if it does not come from the clergy.

The Editor's request for this documentation was probably inspired by "the fact that from the beginning of the liturgical reform here, too, there has been a search for more autonomous and contemporary liturgical forms (often a renewal rather than a reform)". This fact "has moved many people, including some outside the centres approved for experimentation, and particularly young people, who no longer felt at home in either the Church or churches, have again become involved in more or less regular celebrations of the liturgy".[1]

[1] The reply of the Dutch bishops to *prot.* n. 1287/67 of the post-conciliar Council for the Liturgy in May 1968 (*Lit. Jahrbuch* XIX, 96, p. 54). It is curious that this Reply was never printed in the *Notitiae*, the official

In their reply to the questions put to them by the post-conciliar Liturgical Commission the Dutch bishops summed up the situation thus: "One can say that this short period of liturgical reform has also shown an increase in the life of the faith as such, although it is difficult to determine how much of this is due to the reform of the liturgy as such and how much to the whole, very lively and active situation which obtains in Holland at present."[2]

I. The Search for Criteria

The description which follows covers a somewhat arbitrary selection, inspired more or less by the supplementary request of the Editor to provide some critical assessment, if possible. It will be obvious that no one author can give a satisfactory answer here. He can only raise a number of questions. A meaningful evaluation of what is going on in the liturgy requires the contribution of many experts, and not only liturgical experts, each examining what is happening in the liturgy from his own particular angle.

A modest start was made by the Institute for Religious Psychology of Nijmegen University at the request of the Dutch Liturgical Commission. The report on the results of these investigations was discussed at the third symposium on "the Liturgy and the behavioural sciences", organized by the Dutch Liturgical Commission and the Interdiocesan Commission for Pastoral Liturgy (Flanders) in Berg en Dal (Holland) on 23 and 24 November 1968.[3]

The report on "the laborious struggle which marked this third symposium can be found in a special issue of *Tijdschrift voor Liturgie*.[4] This symposium made the participants for the first time understand something of each other's particular language, and this holds not only for the theologians and liturgical experts who were present but also for the sociologists and psychologists.

---

publication of the Congregation for the Liturgy, while the reactions of other hierarchies were.

[2] *Ibid.*

[3] The first symposium was held 29–30 September in Nijmegen on the historico-religious background of the Liturgy; the second on "Religion and Liturgy" was held in Berg en Dal, 27–8 April 1967.

[4] *Tijdschr. v. Lit.* LIII (69), pp. 85–129.

The meagre results clearly show that this investigation was no more than a start. The examination "of the liturgical form given to the celebrations of the Eucharist at week-ends" may well make a further contribution. This question will be examined at conferences organized by K.A.S.K.I. at the week-ends of 26–27 September and 3–4 October 1970.

Perhaps the nature of this inquiry was somewhat different. Its declared purpose was "to get some insight into the nature and composition of what is offered in the liturgy in order to obtain an overall picture of the variety of liturgical service and the degree in which the faithful make use of this service".[5]

The following critical observations are therefore only meant to raise questions about aspects of the liturgy which are perhaps not sufficiently brought out and point out elements that may be overstressed. The critic himself must be careful here not to make the same mistake as so many others who have a go at renewing the liturgy, namely that of underlining the aspect one has discovered for oneself so heavily that no justice is done to the liturgy as a whole, so rich in themes and possible ways of expression and so open to all kinds of approach.

To judge a liturgical service accurately we must always keep in mind the purpose of the service: for whom is it composed, and where is it meant to be celebrated. A service may often appeal to only one type of faithful. There are "faithful who prefer the solemnity of a service to its direct appeal, or silence, concentration and personal reflection to the communal aspect of the celebration".[6] A service will also be judged differently according to whether one has taken part in it, or only read about it, or followed it on radio or television.

But we also know that participants in one and the same service do not usually come away with the same experience. The fact is well known that the next of kin at a funeral or the bride and bridegroom and their families at a wedding practically always agree that it was a fine and moving service, while spectators and

[5] Cf. *Informatie bulletin van het Bisdom Haarlem* IV (70), p. 30.

[6] H. A. J. Wegman, "De avond voor Pasen spelen wij met vuur", in *Bijdragen* XXXI (70), p. 290. This critical appreciation of H. Oosterhuis's pascal service, "In het Voorbijgaan", shows how difficult it is to judge a new liturgical ritual.

official representatives will maintain the opposite. It seems impossible to discover objective criteria.

It is therefore probably more rewarding to find out whether a liturgical service can be *repeated*, so that people can achieve a genuine religious experience again and again. It is just this repetition to which in general so little attention is paid when liturgical celebrations are organized.

In Holland the emphasis is put in many places on the qualities of "experience" and "creativity". "This creativity is put forward as indispensable. To plan, organize, give shape to, and actually perform a liturgical celebration on the basis of the spontaneous contribution of a few or a number of persons is easily given the name and sanction of creativity. The zest and enthusiasm with which this happens is quickly elevated to the level of a creative value when, in actual fact, it is at most a favourable precondition for such creativity."[7]

It is true that this enthusiasm is indispensable, but the actual result of all this work has little value. "It quickly evaporates. The 'artistic' quality is lacking, which means that it often lacks that particular something which rises above what is directly verifiable and for that reason has a lasting appeal."[8]

II. Youth Masses

Yet the repetition of the service is not only promoted by the artistic quality. Youth Masses are much too popular and appeal too much to many, even older, people. In many places in Holland there is such a service at least once a week, particularly when there are several churches in one locality. In such a situation this liturgy for young people is provided by each church on a rota system. In other places, even in the smallest villages, there is still at least once a month a youth Mass and there are churches where, except for the holidays, the young people themselves organize the liturgy once a week.

In general the composition of the youth Mass is seen as an experiment, a possible way towards a more real liturgy, more

[7] E. P. de Jong, "Jongerenliturgie", *Tijdschr. v. Lit.* LIV (70), p. 51.
[8] *Ibid.*, p. 52.

relevant to life. A striking feature is that here music in particular is taken very seriously, and this music, so to speak, carries the liturgy.

As an experiment the youth Mass meets an existing demand for a more religious and political content. It is, nevertheless, not absolutely clear what exactly these religious demands and desires are that must be met. One might wonder whether the liturgy, too, has become a marketable value. Even outside the church "God is apparently good commercial value". One has but to look at the many discs that provoke some kind of religious feeling. Liturgical producers play on this state of affairs and so try to keep the liturgical movement going.

There is, indeed, a widespread wish for a liturgy with a constantly fresh appeal to man, so that he can achieve a genuine experience. The answer to this demand is a liturgy which remains new and creative. But against this tendency there appears the opposite one which turns against any liturgical renewal and wants to fall back on what is old and familiar. Such people maintain that the development is going too fast, that one no longer recognizes the liturgy. These people find great strength in the liturgy, which can be constantly turned into genuine experience, and so they experience a greater tranquillity. They ask for some kind of order within what—to them—is just chaos.

And so we live with many questions, often not explicitly formulated, such as: is the development going too fast? are we not losing certain values? are we not in danger of losing faith itself? Many people demand a clear proclamation of the message of the Lord Jesus Christ, but a proclamation in word and deed, in a language that can be understood, which makes sense in terms of our ordinary everyday life, a proclamation which recognizes the needs of our time, but at the same time the need for religion and for a meaning to life.

Many Dutch pastors try to find a concrete solution to these problems when they celebrate the liturgy. In the search for new forms there are several tendencies, two of which I want to single out: the liturgy for young people, and what I would like to call "collage liturgy".

Youth liturgy does not actually exist. But this is the name given to a number of liturgical compositions which have in common that in one way or another they are aimed at the younger generation and are sometimes composed by the young people themselves in co-operation with the priest.

One can discern two main trends among the many liturgical services which only differ on points of detail. But these differences in detail should be taken seriously because they mean so much to those who compose the service and because they reproduce, in their view, the local character. I wonder, though, whether these differences in detail can be interpreted as a contribution to the renewal of the liturgy. On the other hand, it is significant to the whole situation and this activity of the clergy has to be judged positively in so far as it expresses their concern to offer a sound liturgy.

III. The "Classical" Liturgy for Young People

A first category within the liturgy for young people covers those celebrations which broadly follow the various *Ordines Missae* approved in Holland.[8a] The "youthful" character is mainly determined by the choice of music. This music is marked by a strong rhythm and so corresponds to the kind of music one can hear every day outside the church. In this way those present are encouraged to take part in the singing. In such a service the young people will often take (and sometimes choose) the readings themselves. They also help with the distribution of communion. Occasionally a non-biblical reading is introduced along with the reading from Scripture in order to point the application to the actual situation. The reason is that these services are usually built round one particular theme.[8b] When a youth liturgy is started in a parish, this usually will be the form it takes.

From the positive point of view it must be said that people easily *recognize* their own situation in such services, which makes many feel at ease. Many will find it a positive advantage that the

[8a] The Dutch hierarchy allowed two *Ordines Missae "ad experimentum"* along with the Roman *Ordo Missae*. In the second *Ordo* there are, moreover, eleven canons which were composed in Holland. The official edition appeared as Part I of the Missal: *Ordo Missae* (Hilversum, 1970).

[8b] A survey of the themes used was included with the first issue of the *Werkmap voor Jongerenliturgie*, which is no longer obtainable.

contribution by young people themselves is still limited to the choice of music and their functioning during the service: the reading of Scripture, the bidding prayers and the distribution of communion. The young are considered perfectly capable of making up prayers but some find that their faith is still too much a "searching" faith. They are afraid that this affects the proclamation of the Gospel and the expression of it in prayer.

Another positive advantage is the contribution made by the *young choir*. In actual fact this is the element which carries and pulls together the whole composition of these celebrations. Very soon, if not from the start, an attempt is made to raise the level of the music, although this will also depend on the expertise of the conductor. It is hardly astonishing that this leads to a tendency to "perform" a kind of choral music which, since this comes about too quickly, will diminish the opportunity for popular participation.

The way the repertoire develops shows an inclination to bring back the classical genre of liturgical music. In spite of the fact that this limits participation in the singing by the people, many keep on coming because they like the "atmosphere" and the care given to organizing such services is far greater than with other services.

This form of youth liturgy meets the desire of a large number of people who like to experience their religion in a certain anonymity: within the wider group these people have the opportunity to live their individual piety within the liturgy. This, therefore, continues the individualistic approach to the liturgy. The liturgy has already been influenced by this individualism since the Gothic age. It even penetrated the Church's hymns[9] at that time. During the Renaissance, too, individualism influenced the communal celebration. The liturgy is then seen as an opportunity to take stock of oneself and a sign that one is at peace with the Church.[10]

Nobody will deny the legitimacy of this individualism, but it leaves the hieratic character of the liturgy untouched and "if what is here expected of the liturgy is taken as the norm one would

[9] Cf. A. L. Mayer, "Die Liturgie und der Geist der Gotik", in *Jahrb. f. Liturgiewiss.* VI (1926), pp. 68–97.

[10] Cf. A. L. Mayer, "Renaissance, Humanismus und Liturgie", in *Jahrb. f. Liturgiewiss.* XIV (1934), pp. 123–71.

almost have to say that the public proclamation is so completely attuned to the private sector that the public (political) sector can only be accommodated in a kind of private proclamation".[11]

I would therefore say, with H. Lagerberg, that "it is necessary to make political theology also operative in the normal proclamation and the liturgy. It will always be necessary, no doubt, to try to strike a certain balance between the celebrating and the apostolic character of the liturgy, although this balance may vary.... Liturgy and proclamation must not be reduced to what is purely ethical. The tension between gift and task, between indicative and imperative, between the 'already' and the 'not yet' must always be preserved."[12]

IV. Expression

In youth liturgy the attempt is made not to limit the musical element to singing, side by side with the spoken word. It is increasingly found that purely instrumental music can help considerably to bring life to the service, and the dance, too, is used. By trying out other forms of expression than the word alone it is hoped to avoid a too exclusive moral earnestness. The festive and joyful aspect of the Christian message is conveyed by this use of bodily expression.

There are of course those who maintain that such a show only serves to attract young people, or that this kind of thing should not be done because it has never been done before, or other such remarks. Obviously there will be people who will run out of the service because of this. And yet we see constantly that many people are drawn by this interpretation of the word of Scripture in movements of the body. Man has not only ears to hear with but also eyes to see with. Harvey Cox rightly observes that the medium begins to be part of the message, and that people who have rejected Christian ideas because only presented in some didactic fashion, sometimes find them acceptable when presented in such a festive form.[13]

[11] H. Lagerberg, "Sociaal-kritische pastoraal", in *Theol en Past.* LXVI (70), pp. 105–18.
[12] *Op. cit.*, p. 116.
[13] Harvey Cox, *Het Narrenfeest* (2nd edn., Bilthoven, 1970), p. 69.

All this does not mean that everything offered is necessarily tasteful. The right balance between the musical accompaniment of the spoken word and the bodily movements which interpret it will be found by experimenting. Moreover, many people still have to learn how to understand and handle this kind of expression (both inside and outside the church), and more research is necessary to find out which forms of the dance are suitable. It is therefore natural that, at first, those forms will be chosen that communicate the meaning and feeling more easily.

An example of this was seen in Holland on television. At the end of a Pax Christi march for young people there was a celebration during which the story of creation was "performed" in a way which made it a real event for many viewers. They really saw life begin! In this service there was a great variety of song, play and prayer although the basic structure of the official *Ordo Missae* was totally complied with. While there were spontaneous outbursts such as the singing of "He's a jolly good fellow" addressed to Cardinal Alfrink and Bishop Bluyssen, the celebrant also managed to unite all those present in an impressive silent prayer.

It is of course debatable whether every liturgical service is suitable for transmission by television. What is possible in a church or hall does not always come across on television. The liturgical experts have not yet done enough work to find out the real possibilities and requirements in this medium. Too often the only criterion is that it is "a special event". If this is the only motive for televising the liturgy it is hardly satisfactory.

The liturgy must not only fulfil certain conditions (I am not talking about rubrics here), but the environment, too. For instance, can the interior of the building itself contribute to the service so that the viewer can experience this service in a personal way? One can also underline the services by the use of particular bits of film, as happened when St Francis's Song of the Sun was illustrated with images taken from nature.

[14] One of the other possibilities for radio and television is the so-called studio-Mass. The Catholic radio showed this form of eucharist on Friday nights during the Lent of 1970 on the radio. The reactions showed that listeners genuinely felt themselves involved in this celebration and that in some cases they also went to communion. Attempts to achieve this also on television have not been fully worked out. I do not know of any critical evaluation of all this by theologians or liturgical experts.

On the other hand, one should not transmit a service where, for instance, the choir of young people only serves as a stop-gap. A service, too, which is so special that it can only become intelligible by means of a text which links the various parts, is not suitable for transmission. The intellectual character of such services is sometimes even underlined by a lack of movement and variety.

This last point shows that we must not look for renewal only in the structure. If one dares ignore some details that appear in the Roman *Ordo Missae*,[15] there is room enough within the broad framework of this *Ordo* for a celebration that leads to an intense solidarity, reinforces the sharing of feelings and convictions, and so emphasizes the oneness of all. Then the ritual can again become "a communicating process where the participants can experience in a particular way their common inspiration, feelings and desires in view of the common purpose".[16]

V. Youth Ministry

Side by side with this first kind of youth liturgy and along with it we see the rise of a movement among young people and pastors concerned with young people which is sometimes called "youth liturgy" but which is in fact more than liturgy, and for some even no longer liturgy. What is probably meant by liturgy then is a strictly sacramental liturgy. In their dissatisfaction with the traditional structure of the eucharist, both priests and young people find that the liturgy is still too detached, too individualistic, too little committed. They feel that a liturgy which has no consequences for life is not real. This movement has helped to rediscover the apostolic character of the eucharist. This has led to a stressing of the apostolic character of other celebrations. It comes out in the expanded formulas for the dismissal, although these

[15] There is no clarity at all about the reasons why the Roman documents continue to maintain their "rubricism". This does not only limit the possibilities the liturgy can offer, but it also prevents priests from acquiring a personal attitude to the liturgy which might show their personal commitment and their own personal approach.

[16] B. J. De Clerq, "Liturgische gemeenschap: sociologische of geloofsgemeenschap", in *Tijdschr. v. Lit.* LIV (70), p. 9.

sometimes have an ethical import and often are a very short summary of the sermon.

The liturgy was made to fulfil the need to bring the assembled people to a more committed Christianity. Here the proclamation seemed the most appropriate element. This brought a change in the "service of the word". Its content became something different. It was used mainly to make the faithful aware of existing needs in the world, and with an appeal to Scripture, those present were given to understand that these needs contained a mission for them as Christians. It then becomes almost obvious that situations described by modern authors are given priority over readings from the Bible. And when these readings from Scripture are given, it is usually in a more popular and free translation.

This choice of readings reinforces the contribution made by the young. Here they are on home ground, and frequently better informed about modern literature than many priests. Moreover, if there are prayers, these young people will express their own struggle with the problems of the world or their own search for the faith.

All this is accepted by priests because they find here a better opportunity to speak about the relation between Christianity and the great needs of the world in the sermon which they usually reserve for themselves. Such priests will emphasize the prophetic character of their office.

Sometimes this youth liturgy leads to a youth ministry, sometimes it is this kind of ministry which leads to a youth liturgy. Those who participate in these services are encouraged to take part in activities with an immediate or distant aim. Thus many young people become involved in such activities while at the same time they get equally involved in such services. Basically they dislike making any distinction between their activities and the liturgy.

All this seems to appeal to great numbers of them. Their urge to build a better world to live in is thus given a new dimension. They "celebrate" their activities, and their activities are "sanctified" by the people who take part in their services. Unfortunately, in some cases there is no dialogue with adults and other priests. There is no demand for guidance.

In this context H. Fortmann's remarks are important: "In the pulpit there is talk of Vietnam and democratization because one has no longer anything to say about God, not only because religious experience is lacking but also because the writings of the great spiritual authors and mystics, who had this experience, are no longer known. This religious penury—sometimes combined with fierce theological discussions—might possibly be connected with the fact that our senses are blocked."[17] Then the proceedings become the proceedings of an in-group which leads to isolation. And so the impression is given that one's own ideas are sacred.

VI. Play and Proclamation

To avoid the danger pointed out by Fortmann the youth services also make use of the dance, slides and the short film.[18] An attempt is made to appeal to all the senses for the proclamation of this message of humanity, of brotherhood and common destiny. But the use of these other means of expression seems to be limited to illustration. Often it is not a real play. As P. L. Berger said: "In a play one passes from one period of time into another."[19] And he goes on: "The play always sets up an enclave within the 'serious' social life of every day as well as an enclave within its chronology. This holds equally for a play that produces pain rather than joy."[20]

Precisely because these young people do not know how to use such a play the eucharistic part of the celebration gets into difficulties. The eucharist is increasingly reduced to a short appendix to the service, as if one did not know what to do with it. The eucharistic prayer becomes shorter, and many no longer recognize the narrative of the institution. Often the words of the institution stand isolated in the middle of a prayer which looks more like a speech than a prayer. This makes the consecration look like a kind of magic.

[17] Han Fortmann, *Oosterse Renaissance* (Bilthoven, 1970), p. 13.
[18] The work-group, "Beeld en Dienst", has published a pamphlet, *In gesprek met film en dia*, with practical instructions for the use of transparencies or short films in church worship (Stichting Filmsentrum, Steynlaan 8, Hilversum).
[19] P. L. Berger, *Er zijn nog altijd engelen* (Utrecht, 1969), p. 74.
[20] *Ibid.*

And yet, they cling to the "breaking of the bread". Some are afraid of letting it go in case this frightens people away. Others accept that this gesture is an essential part of the Sunday service. Others again see it as a moment when everyone present can take an active part. But, above all, this gesture is experienced and proclaimed as expressing brotherhood. Unfortunately, in some cases the impression is given that the eucharist means only that, even though some, particularly older, people will receive communion there in the context of their own piety.

The great value of these services lies in the force of their proclamation. They convey a Christian summons to get involved in this world, in everyday life, and they firmly point to the overriding urgency of its needs.

It has to be said that occasionally this summons is felt as a kind of coercion. Sometimes too little room is left for personal initiative and for a certain anonymity in the exercise of brotherly love. The indication of the world's needs is sometimes coloured in rather narrow political terms, and so provokes resistance. Recently a typical reaction was found on the cover of a small handbook for a youth liturgy: "I go to church in a certain sense to find rest, far away from problems outside the church. In the church I try to find solutions for the difficulties I have to face outside."[21]

One can say of this second kind of youth liturgy that its main value lies in the intense preparation for these services and the activities connected with them. They certainly contribute to a clearer understanding of what the liturgy is and means to be. On the other hand, they provoke a lot of questions, particularly they do not underrate the play and symbolism.

Sometimes one hears the observation: "They must not go any further with driving out the symbol and turning it all into a game." For it is the symbol that creates space and freedom so that everyone can take part in his own way. The symbol fully accepts the earthly reality, but it brings at the same time a deeper reality, God.

The proclamation is often strongly tied to a place and depends on only one person. This is of course inevitable in liturgical worship. But this stringent concentration on the locality

[21] Stencilled copy, Jongerenmis Voorburg.

frightens people off because the Church's faith stretches beyond the present into the past and the future. This place-bound character can also lead to isolation and alienation. Sometimes it becomes painfully clear when the priest in charge leaves and no successor can be found.

This kind of liturgy rightly reacts against the individualistic approach to the sacraments which used to be fostered by the fact that liturgical actions were mainly seen as acting *ex opere operato* (the mere performance of the ritual). But these services also raise the question whether the tension between human commitment and God's coming can be truly and always experienced.

Hence it is sometimes suggested that on Sundays people who mainly want to celebrate man's commitment to the kingdom of God should only be given a service of the word, with all the value of a liturgy, including as a consequence the Sunday obligation.

There clearly is a demand for a proclamation of a Christianity committed to the world, both in word and in actual experience. But such a proclamation should be preceded by a clear explanation of what human existence is about.

All this is still far from being realized. And this is why, for many people, the eucharist, in its dimension of contact with God, cannot become a direct experience. When these services of the word are going to be offered to the people as one aspect of the total expression of the liturgy, they will without doubt enrich Christianity.

VII. The Family Mass

This demand for a liturgy that is more concerned with a contemporary relevant proclamation of the faith than with the celebration of a salvation that has already been received has also led to a very different phenomenon: the family Mass. The name of this eucharistic celebration was prompted by the desire to have a eucharist which aims at both children of the age of primary education and their parents. "The liturgy of the church-of-the-grown-ups meant little to them."[22] "The 'service of the word' begins therefore with a small play, a simple affair with mime and

[22] P. van der Brugge and J. Poel, "De Gezinsmis in de Roermondse Kathedraal", *G. en S.* 70/3 (May 1970), p. 60.

dialogue, acted by children from different schools, dressed up in colourful garments (one can use practically anything), and enlivened with some suitable music, a little dance and a small set. The theme is taken from the gospel of the Sunday or the liturgical season."[23]

Here, too, one finds the difficulty how to link it with the proper celebration of the eucharist. "Sometimes it is obvious (when the story deals with a festive meal), sometimes it is difficult. The adaptation is then likely to look rather artificial."[24]

These services are also often seen as good opportunities to let the parents share in the religious knowledge the children have received at school, while the parents have a chance of finding out what the children are being taught.

These family Masses seem to have increased in recent times. Particularly young parents are very interested because they are then often involved in the preparation, just as the young people in the youth liturgy. Great care will, however, have to be taken to prevent the whole experiment from becoming bogged down in infantilism.

As long as such services are limited to first communion everybody will accept them, because here the child is the centre of attention. But when adults receive only this kind of proclamation, it is the parents that will get bored, not the children, even though such parents will remain interested at first by the sight of their own child functioning in the liturgy.

It will remain true that "before everything else adults must really try to celebrate the liturgy with one another. Only the child who learns to experience the liturgy as real in this communal event will really profit by some instruction about it. To proceed in the opposite direction will certainly mean that both adult and child will drift into lack of authenticity or intellectualism."[25]

VIII. Collage Liturgy

Collage liturgy shows a great deal of similarity with certain forms of the youth liturgy. But it differs in that it is not primarily

[23] *Ibid.*, p. 61. [24] *Ibid.*, pp. 62–3.

[25] J. H. Huyts, *Godsdienstige opvoeding in een overgangstijd* (=Ser. Geestelijke volksgezondheid, 20, Utrecht), p. 16.

aimed at the young and that it looks from the start for a special structure, at first still within the framework of the *Ordo Missae* but soon outside it.

In such services people try to confront facts gleaned from the press with the Gospel. It becomes a kind of dialogue. In this way people try to achieve a contemporary and relevant understanding and experience of the Gospel.

This kind of service deliberately aims at the "play" and therefore makes use of all possible means to bring this about. Thus we read in the introduction to *Dansend in het donker. Een samenkomst vanwege kerstmis* (Dancing in the dark. A Christmas gathering):[26] Whereas in a circus we would find a passage going from the ring to the stables, there is in this church no curtain but a wide wall of newspapers reaching up to the ceiling—the world of people running straight into it, being surprised by it, shrinking back from it and looking up to it. In the middle of the wall a white square is left free for projection. In front of the wall there stands a tree, not a Christmas tree, but one made of laths, the tree of our life.... A close look reveals somewhere on the stem the head of Christ. On both sides there is a long wall-paper—with nothing on it as yet." The stage-direction for another service says: "A play of just movement could show all that comes out of man once he is actually living, all the good as well as the evil he initiates. There is room here for some projection and music, to create 'environment' in some small way. Birth, particularly, should be pictured."[27] Dramatic action is also put to use. Thus a direction says: "Somebody who can model, for instance, a potter, is busy with clay, and the light is made to focus on what he is doing with his hands. Soft background music may accompany this action. Somebody says something."[28]

These liturgical services require much and intense preparation, and involve many people. It is not easy to celebrate one such service in the same way in different places. An introduction to three Christmas liturgies states that "these three Christmas

[26] *Een kerstdienst samengesteld door H. Verbeek in samenwerking met de liturgische werkgroep van de Studentenparochie Nijmegen* (unpublished).

[27] J. Duin and H. Verbeek, *Planken voor een stal, boom, stal, geboorte. Drie Kerst-liturgieën* (Hilversum, 1970), p. 63.

[28] *Planken voor een stal*, p. 60.

liturgies contain texts, songs and scenes to be acted, with which a midnight service can be composed according to the requirements of the place or the group".[29]

In practice it is clear that these liturgical celebrations are only composed for special occasions, like Christmas, Easter, or some jubilee. The first service of this kind known to me is that composed by Jan Duin (words) and Jan Raas (music) on the occasion of the 150th anniversary of the minor seminary of Hageveld in Heemstede under the title, "Whose bread one eats, his word one speaks" (Dutch version of "he who pays the piper calls the tune"). In this sober service the collage was limited to a service of the word, consisting of a recital in which several people spoke a number of texts, interrupted by music, while everybody joined in the acclamations. The collage was limited to relating a text from Scripture to the present situation.

I have seen the misery
Of my people that live in Egypt,
And heard them cry out in the camp
Where slave-drivers oppress them.
I know their sufferings:
I know the Jew suffering in his ghetto
And see how he has been hurt;
I know the Negro in his hovel
And know that he is not allowed to live;
I know man in India
And see that he has nothing to eat;
I know the white man—
And feel how isolated he is
In the working-class quarter of Chicago,
In cities that are but stone,
With people that are but flesh.
I know you all—
Men who love and suffer,
Men who hope and fear,
Men of good and evil,
Men fragile—like bread.[31]

[29] *Ibid.*, p. 3.
[30] This service has not been published and was composed in 1967.
[31] *Planken voor een stal*, pp. 4–5.

The way the most important celebrations of the faith are related to the life of every day is very different in the one already mentioned, "Dancing in the dark", and in an Easter service by Herman Verbeek, entitled, "God, Great Fish, do not stand still".[32] A similar approach is found in "Planks for a stall". In their introduction to the latter the authors say: "Other people are waiting for a new programme which will probably look less attractive but on the other hand more authentic. An increasing number of people want to put together their own kind of celebration. Here they look elsewhere for ideas and suggestions. It will depend on their own disposition and circumstances whether the atmosphere of their Christmas night is going to be playful or serious, festive or sober, in the mystic mood or realistic."[33]

It is impossible to describe these more expanded collages. One has to share in them in order to get into them and understand them as a whole. One might say that people seriously "play" with Scripture and the life of every day. The texts are strongly associative. The participants are encouraged as far as possible to take an active share in the proceedings during which at some given points of the service the choice is left to each. An example of the way this is done follows here:

Ladies and gentlemen, now we have a pause.
We cannot go on.
For this is the night,
Not of a fine cross,
But of a true cross,
Of a truth
That must be done.
Therefore we ourselves must fill
The emptiness of this pause.
Here, in the middle, stands a table,
And on it lies a book
In which you can write bidding prayers.
Over there stands a stone jar
In which you can put some money for Lent.
In the left corner of the church

[32] This service also has not been published.
[33] *Planken voor een stal*, p. 3.

You'll find a stall,
Where you can send picture postcards
Of this night:
"Greetings from the students' church
In Nijmegen—Easter vigil 1968".
Finally, on the right-hand side
There is a stall where you can put
Your signature under four letters
That will be posted during this night.[34]

The texts are sometimes difficult to understand because they are part of a play. A given image prompts a number of thoughts associated with it. These are more easily understood when one reads them because then the allusions to a given biblical text or a concrete situation follow each other less quickly than during the actual performance. Much gets lost in mere listening and it is often the quantity which creates the atmosphere. People who are not accustomed to the manipulation of language will find it too difficult or fail to grasp the meaning of the whole. An attempt is made to speak a kind of "second language", but I doubt whether this always succeeds. It is, of course, possible that the authors do not mean every single sentence and every single word to be understood.

IX. The Problem of the Language of the Liturgy

Collage-liturgy raises the problem of what is the appropriate language to be used in the liturgy. This problem already arose when the Latin texts were first translated. In Holland one meets with a double criticism. It is said that "certain forms of linguistic usage do not belong in the church, partly because the ordinary man cannot understand them, partly because they evoke an atmosphere which is thought to be irreconcilable with the language of the Church".[35]

On the other hand, P. H. H. Winkels observes: "Is there not something to be said for trying to broaden the linguistic usage of the ordinary people and so to introduce them to forms of

[34] *God, grote vis, blijf niet staan.* Een samenkomst vanwege Pasen, by H. Verbeek, ms. pp. 38–9.

[35] P. H. H. Winkels, "Hoort intellectuele dichtertaal nu wel of niet in de kerk thuis?", in *G. en S.* 70/3, p. 50.

religious experience which up till then were beyond their reach? Why should the formulation of the mysterious element, which is in fact a feature of any belief, be expected to be so crystal-clear? Is there no room for some human mysteries when we are in the presence of the great Mystery? The one criticism we can make of a hymn-writer is that he has no real grip of the mystery, not that he honestly tries."[36]

It is certainly not merely a disguised longing for a "church language" which lies behind these questions, but rather the problem of how to put the Gospel into words that are recognizable. The collage-services have certainly made a contribution to a new language for the liturgy.

These services are particularly valuable for those people who only come on special occasions. They are an attempt to play along with the problems as they see them, and to show the human face of Jesus. This is why one particular aspect of salvation is emphasized: the commitment to one's fellow men, as Christ showed and fulfilled it.

Many people experience these services as an event that really happens to them, and takes them out of themselves. But there is also a certain ambiguity. There is too little narrating of the kind that recalls, reminds, and thus celebrates. S. Ijsseling once remarked in another context: "Some people see the truth as a self-contained piece of territory, where they themselves live and to which they invite others; or as some kind of acquired possession in which, out of sheer zeal, they want others to share.... Salvation is 'known' in one way or another, and the telling of the saving story is but a consequence of this knowledge. That such a theology is bound to end up with the death of God and total incredibility is for us the writing on the wall."[37]

This collage-liturgy has a powerful influence on people. The more common liturgical forms unfortunately often fail here. For many faith has been for long a purely intellectual affair with little room for the emotions. The collage-services act strongly on this emotional element, but do they really create "the inner wholeness of the person and that framework for the whole of

[36] *Op. cit.*, p. 51.
[37] S. Ijsseling, "De verwevenheid van universiteit en theologie", in *Tijdschr. v. Lit.* X (70), p 130.

life where all things are coherently brought together?" God is "known", but nothing is told about him. "This story is written down in books, and these books themselves are again an essential part of the story. Scripture is the literary deposit, sediment, of a constantly repeated song of praise and thanksgiving, of a story constantly told afresh, and of an order founded in the past."[38]

The service creates a bond between all present. "Everyone lets his glass be filled with wine, and has a second glass.... When all have drunk their fill, one hears above the general noise: 'Thus Jesus performed his first miracle, in Cana of Galilee, and revealed there his glory. His disciples believed in him' (John 2. 11)."[39] This bond evokes the Lord's Supper, at which the Covenant with God and with men was celebrated.

"Before a new liturgy", says Stephen Neill, "can have any hope of lasting success, it is essential that both the makers of liturgies and those who use them should have a clear understanding of the theological purpose that underlies the work."[40] In Holland people are looking for a new shape of the liturgy, are experimenting with gusto, and there is a genuine commitment to the fellow man. But the reasons and motives which have prompted all this might be brought out more clearly in a theological reflection which does not underrate the emotional experience.

[38] *Ibid*., p. 129.
[39] H. Verbeek, ms., p. 73.
[40] S. Neill, "Does our Church need a New Reformation?: An Anglican Reply", *Concilium* (April 1970), p. 75 (American edn., Vol. 54).

Translated by Theo Westow

Biographical Notes

CORNELIS DIPPEL was born 28 March 1902 at Bilt (Netherlands), and is a Protestant. He studied at the University of Gröningen. Doctor of chemistry and hon. doctor of theology, he has directed a research group in photochemistry at the Philips Laboratory at Eindhoven. Among his published works is: *Kerk en wereld in de crisis* (The Hague, 1966²).

ANDREW GREELEY was born 5 February 1928 at Oak Park (U.S.A.) and ordained in 1954. He studied in the United States at St Mary of the Lake Seminary and at Chicago University. Master of arts, licentiate in theology, doctor of sociology, he is lecturer in the Department of Sociology at Chicago University, and Senior Study Director of the National Opinion Research Center at the same university. Among his published works are *The Hesitant Pilgrim: American Catholicism after the Council* (London, 1960) and *A Future to Hope in* (New York, 1969).

HELMET HUCKE was born 12 March 1927 at Kassel (Germany) and is a Catholic. He studied at the High School of Music at the University of Freiburg in Breisgau. Doctor of philosophy, he is assistant professor of Church music at the Institute of Liturgy at Trier. Among his published works is: "Das 'munus ministeriale' der Musik im Christlichen Kult" in *Kirchenmusik nach dem Konzil* (Freiburg, 1967).

EUGENE C. KENNEDY, M.M., studied at Maryknoll College, Illinois. Doctor of philosophy, he is professor of psychology at Loyola University, Chicago. He edits a Bulletin, *You* (research on personal and spiritual fulfilment). Among his books are *Fashion Me a People* and *Comfort My People.*

JUAN LLOPIS was born 17 July 1932 at Barcelona and ordained in 1958. He studied in Rome at the Gregorian University and at the Liturgical Institute of St Anselm, and in Spain at the University of Salamanca and the Faculty of Theology at Barcelona. Doctor of theology, he is professor of liturgy at the University of Salamanca and at the Higher Institute of Pastoral Studies at Madrid. Among his published works is: *La Sagrada*

Escritura, fuente de inspiración de la liturgia de difuntos del antiguo rito hispánico (Barcelona, 1965).

EUGENE H. MALY was born 6 September 1920 at Cincinnati and ordained in 1943. He studied at Cincinnati University and, in Rome, at the Angelicum and the Biblical Institute. Doctor of theology and of Sacred Scripture, he is professor of Holy Scripture at Mount St Mary's Seminary in Cincinnati. Among his published works are: *The World of David and Solomon* (New York, 1966) and *The Book of Wisdom* (New York, 1962).

GÜNTER ROMBOLD was born 2 January 1925 at Stuttgart and ordained in 1949. He studied at the Universities of Linz and Munich. Doctor of philosophy and of theology, he is professor at the Academic Gymnasium of Linz. Among his publications are: *Das Wesen der Person nach John Henry Newman* and *Der Mensch vor Gott* (Linz, 1966).

HERMAN SCHMIDT, S.J., was born 26 June 1912 at Roermond and ordained in 1940. He studied at the University of Nijmegen and, in Rome, at the Oriental Institute, the Institute of Archaeology, the Institute of Sacred Music and at the School of Palaeography of the Vatican. Licentiate in philosophy and doctor of theology (1946), he is professor of liturgy at the Gregorian University and at the Liturgical Institute of St Anselm in Rome. Among his publications are: *Introductio in Liturgiam Occidentalem* (Rome, 1965[3]) and *Constitutie over de H. Liturgie* (Antwerp, 1964).

JÖRG SPLETT was born 29 August 1936 at Magdeburg and is a Catholic. Doctor of philosophy, he is scientific assistant and assistant professor at the University of Munich. Among his published works are: *Der Mensch in seiner Freiheit* (Mainz, 1967) and *Sakrament der Wirklichkeit* (Würzburg, 1968).

(ERNEST) JOHN TINSLEY was born 22 March 1919 at Maghull, Lancs., and ordained priest in the Anglican Church in 1942. He studied in England at Durham University and at Westcott House, Cambridge. Master of arts and bachelor of theology, he is professor of theology at Leeds University. Among his published works are: *The Imitation of God in Christ* (London, 1960) and *The Gospel according to Luke* (Cambridge, 1965).

ANTOINE VERGOTE was born 8 December 1921 at Courtrai and is a priest. He studied at Louvain University and at the Sorbonne. Doctor of philosophy and of theology, he is professor of the psychology of religion at Louvain University. Among his published works are: *Psychologie religieuse* (Brussels, 1964) and *La relation pastorale individuelle* (Paris, 1967).

International Publishers of CONCILIUM

ENGLISH EDITION
Herder and Herder, Inc.
New York, U.S.A.

Burns & Oates Ltd.
P.O. Box 497
London, S.W.7

DUTCH EDITION
Uitgeverij Paul Brand, N.V.
Hilversum, Netherlands

FRENCH EDITION
Maison Mame
Tours/Paris, France

JAPANESE EDITION (PARTIAL)
Nansôsha
Tokyo, Japan

GERMAN EDITION
Verlagsanstalt Benziger & Co., A.G.
Einsiedeln, Switzerland

Matthias Grunewald-Verlag
Mainz, W. Germany

SPANISH EDITION
Ediciones Cristianidad
Salamanca, Spain

PORTUGUESE EDITION
Livraria Morais Editoria, Ltda.
Lisbon, Portugal

ITALIAN EDITION
Editrice Queriniana
Brescia, Italy

POLISH EDITION (PARTIAL)
Pallottinum
Poznań, Poland